A Monk's Guide to Finding Joy

# A Monk's Guide to Finding Joy

HOW TO TRAIN YOUR MIND AND
TRANSFORM YOUR LIFE

## H. E. Khangser Rinpoche

Foreword by His Holiness the Dalai Lama

Wisdom

Wisdom Publications
132 Perry Street
New York, NY 10014 USA
wisdomexperience.org

*Library of Congress Cataloging-in-Publication Data*
Names: Tenzin Tsultrim Palden, Khangser Rinpoche, 1975– author.
Title: A monk's guide to finding joy: how to train your mind and transform your life /
    H.E. Khangser Rinpoche.
Description: First edition. | New York: Wisdom Publications, 2024. |
    Includes bibliographical references and index.
Identifiers: LCCN 2023052656 (print) | LCCN 2023052657 (ebook) |
    ISBN 9781614299158 (paperback) | ISBN 9781614299301 (ebook)
Subjects: LCSH: Spiritual life—Buddhism. | Blo-sbyong.
Classification: LCC BQ7805 .T44 2024 (print) | LCC BQ7805 (ebook) |
    DDC 294.3/44–dc23/eng/20231117
LC record available at https://lccn.loc.gov/2023052656
LC ebook record available at https://lccn.loc.gov/2023052657

ISBN 978-1-61429-915-8     ebook ISBN 978-1-61429-930-1

28 27 26 25 24
5  4  3  2  1

Cover art and design by Marc Whitaker / MTW Design.
Interior design by Gopa & Ted2. Inc.

Please visit fscus.org.

To my encouraging master, who taught me, inspired me,
and acted as a powerful role model in my life.

To my loving mom, who wholeheartedly supports my ideas,
regardless of how ambitious they are.

To my hopeful father, whose contagious optimism motivates me,
even when things are not going well.

To my supportive brother, whose dedication to caring
for our parents enables me to roam free and focus
on my mission to help others.

I once had a clay pot, now I do not.

This case illustrates every composite thing.

It exemplifies human bodies of leisure and opportunity.

This being so, I Mila the yogin

Will press on in my practice without distraction.

This clay pot so important, the whole of my wealth,

Becomes my lama in the moment it breaks,

Teaching impermanence, how amazing!

—MILAREPA, in *The Life of Milarepa,*
translated by Andrew Quintman

# Contents

# Foreword
## by His Holiness the Dalai Lama

Khangser Rinpoche is a knowledgeable monk who has studied at one of the great Tibetan monastic centers of learning re-established in South India, Sera Jey Monastery. He graduated with distinction as a *geshe lharampa* and went on to train at Gyuto Tantric College, where he now holds a position of eminence.

In addition to his learning as a scholar of the ancient Indian Nalanda tradition preserved in Tibetan monasteries, Khangser Rinpoche is also at home in the modern world. He has followers in many different countries and speaks fluent English.

In this book, *A Monk's Guide to Finding Joy,* Rinpoche shares what he has learned in practical terms. He's not thinking in terms of past and future lives, but of how we can find joy in this very life. If we could remember that humanity is one, and if we were able to live in harmony and help one another, how good that would be.

As human beings, one of the most important things we have in common is a wish simply to be happy—none of us want to be miserable. The key to fulfilling this wish lies in training the mind. Not only can we tame our unruly emotions, but we can also learn to think in a more positive and healthy way. By achieving peace of mind and cultivating a warm heart, we can develop courage and inner strength so that when we are faced with difficulties, we can easily cope with them.

Rinpoche has illustrated his book with stories from many different sources that make what he has to say not only easy to understand, but also a pleasure to read. I am confident readers will take delight in this book and invite them to share the joy they find in it with others.

January 28, 2024

# Preface

THE CATALYST that led me to write this book was a woman who thanked me for saving her life. She thought the only way out of her relentless anguish was suicide. She read one of my books as a last-ditch effort, and after reading it, she felt optimistic and hopeful about her life. That inspired her to not just keep living but to accept reality as it is and change her mindset for the better. Yet it wasn't me that saved her life; it was the culmination of the wisdom and compassion that I've learned from over forty years of studying and practicing the teachings of the Buddha. A buddha isn't a god. A buddha is a person who is awake to the truth of the way things are. This insight into the truth, and the practices that help you cultivate this awareness, transforms suffering into wisdom and compassion, and ultimately joy.

Even though I have an honorary title in the Buddhist community, I'm just a human with the same challenges as everyone else. I really can empathize with the struggles that all people face. And when I consider the suffering presently permeating life in our society, I feel an urgent desire to help, especially given the recent rise in depression and anxiety, which hits young people and women the hardest. The current state of our existence has increased fear, grief, sadness, anger, insecurity, division, and loneliness. Personally, I can vouch for the teachings of the Buddha. I practice his teachings myself and can say with one hundred percent certainty that they work. Doing charity projects, building a monastery, and offering instructions worldwide have been the results of my following this path. Even though I am very busy with philanthropic endeavors, I'm happy. I hope for you to be happy too!

Writing this book started as a seed of hope for you, precious reader. Together with my volunteer team from Dipkar Vajrayana Institute, we pulled three of my unpublished manuscripts and carefully outlined them. We then weeded through the outlines for nuggets of wisdom that could help people struggling during these uncertain times. Once this book was outlined, it slowly took form over the course of a year. I headed many online quality-control meetings, which challenged the team. We had to meet across vastly different time zones and make space in our busy schedules to discuss content details. I do not have a personal income, but thanks to the generous monetary donations we received, we were able to hire a professional editor to help guide us through the writing process. I feel fortunate to have found a fantastic publishing company that encourages wisdom and the aspiration to help people live well. Now that the book is a reality, I hope you enjoy it. My primary focus throughout this time has been how I can help you, the reader, live a happy life. May the words on these pages open your mind and heart and bless you, as well as those in your lives, with a joyful existence.

# Introduction

I FEEL SO grateful that my life has been graced with good fortune. In May 1975, in Kathmandu, Nepal, I was reborn as Sonam Topgyai. In Tibetan, my name means Merit with Increasing Strength. I was delivered to a dedicated mom with a kind heart and an optimistic dad who encouraged me to do my best. I was very close with my mom. Her compassionate heart always astounded me. Once, when I was seven years old, she risked her life by embarking on a long journey across rough, perilous terrain just to visit me at my school in northern India. By then, I had already been studying for two years and recognized as the eighth Khangser, which means Yellow House in Tibetan.

One reason why I was recognized as the reincarnation of this spiritual teacher is because word got out that I remembered my past life. I would often talk with my mom about my vivid past life memories of riding a white horse and running a monastery. She always suspected I was special. Even when she was pregnant with me, she sensed that I would go on and do great and helpful things. It was no surprise to her that I was recognized as the eighth incarnate Khangser Rinpoche by the search party from Sera Jey Monastery. When they discovered me at five years of age, I wasn't clear about what was going on around me, but I was clear about certain things from the past. I had a clear recollection of what my previous monastery looked like, particularly the surrounding mountains. I also felt well acquainted with monastic practices, such as sitting in lotus position with my hands poised in the teaching *mudra*. Even though I was uncertain of the role I was to play, it became clear fast that the title Rinpoche held a lot of importance.

Once they confirmed my previous existence, I was escorted to the monastery in southern India, where an enthronement ceremony was held for me. Students and monastics greeted me, claiming that I had been, and was now again, their teacher. At that moment, I felt so fortunate and blessed. Shortly after, I was assigned a caretaker by the name of Kelsang Chodak. He not only acted as a caring parent but answered my questions about life and the Buddhist path. He was not the only strong influential adult in my early years of study; at age eight, while attending school in India, I met the Tibetan teacher I refer to as my master. His name was Khensur Lobsang Tsering, and he was a former abbot of Sera Jey Monastery. I had an intuitive feeling that he was destined to teach me, so I made certain to talk with him. When I asked him whether I should follow the Buddhist path or not, he laughed joyfully in response. He knew that this path was a narrow, personal path that one must choose to take without any outside pressure. Pleased with his answer, and feeling grateful to find him, I gave him my prized little ceramic statue of the well-known Tibetan philosopher Lama Tsongkhapa. I appreciated finding such an excellent teacher.

My teacher was a calm, philosophical, intelligent person who was never rash. When making decisions, he'd carefully consider all the factors involved before deciding what to do. Once he made up his mind to do something, he'd work tirelessly toward his objective. I never once saw him dissuaded by unkind gossip or discouraging remarks, despite his revolutionary goals. He was the one who insisted that our Buddhist institutions adopt a strictly vegetarian diet, regardless of the Tibetan monks' love of meat. He also revolutionized our monastery by incorporating health care and formal education into our traditional monastic system. He doggedly worked toward updating our antiquated ways of thinking and doing things while steadily following the Buddhist path.

During the Cultural Revolution in China, a hostile campaign was waged to eliminate Tibetan religion, culture, identity, and traditions. During that time, my master was imprisoned for several years simply because he taught others a way to end their suffering. Nevertheless, despite his imprisonment, he refused to harbor any ill will toward his captors. Instead, he prayed in earnest to be freed so he could continue to help liberate others from their anguish. He never grumbled or griped over this incident or complained of any ills. Instead, he insisted that the purpose of his life was to benefit others. His greatest wish was to help ease the mental and emotional difficulties common to human existence.

My master and I shared this goal, as we did many core beliefs. We had a close bond—so close that just prior to his passing, he conveyed to me that he would be dying soon. He conveyed this not in words, but by his silent response when I asked him to pray while I was away. He knew, and I too became aware, that he'd not be around to do so.

At age ninety-three my teacher passed away, but his mission did not. His modern way of seeing life, his wisdom, and his teachings live on inside of me. I share his revolutionary spirit and his appreciation of deep philosophic views. He helped me comprehend my role as Rinpoche. Like my master, my purpose is to serve others. For eight lifetimes I have made it my mission to help people find the right path, to offer my emotional support, and to provide resources for those who are materially vulnerable. My teacher pointed out that I'm indebted to multitudes of people who have shown me generosity and support—not just in this lifetime, but over many lifetimes. He urged me to pay back this karmic debt by giving assistance to others and expecting nothing in return.

Thanks to the encouragement of my teachers, fellow monastics, caretakers, family, and master, not one moment of my life goes by without the thought of paying back the generosity of others. I owe so much! That is why I have studied long and hard to obtain the very highest *geshe* degree of monastic scholarship within the Tibetan Geluk tradition, a doctorate degree in Tantric Buddhism, and mastery in the Nyingma Buddhist tradition. I've dedicated my entire life to providing spiritual medicine for what ails a broken spirit. I am on a mission to help as many as I am able. Once, a woman believed so heavily in my mission that even though she was of little means, she gave me the only thing she had of great worth, her gold wedding band. She insisted I keep it. I never sold that band; I keep it as a precious reminder of just how much I owe this world and its inhabitants. This sort of kind generosity is an inspiration to me. Because of people like her, I have developed successful charities and research projects worldwide. All to help alleviate the suffering I witness.

Some suffering that I've witnessed I can't shake. I recall the time I saw a frail, ragged man searching in the garbage for a scrap of food. He found one small piece of bread saturated in filth but ravenously scarfed it down as if he hadn't eaten in weeks. Incidents like this fuel my efforts to give materially. Some people don't even have the means to obtain the basic things needed to live. They lack food, clean water, and shelter. Without these basics, how can someone even begin to think of working on their spiritual improvement? I witness others who have so much wealth yet are impoverished on the inside. They suffer with deep, suicidal depression and struggle with negative emotions such as hatred and greed. Some people I have encountered feel so desperate for inner relief that they take their own lives. Their pain compels me to write books and start research projects that address clear, simple methods to alleviate mental suffering and its associated physical ills. Furthermore, to prevent this sort of inner turmoil, I've set up free in-person and online classes and meditation sessions to impart the helpful wisdom that I have learned.

It seems safe to say that all humans on this earth desperately want happiness. Not just fleeting happiness, but steady, reliable joy. Of late, we have been attempting to capture happiness by any means—especially by making technological advances and relying on consumerism. But happiness cannot, and never will, exist outside of us. It is, without a doubt, an inside job.

I would like to help you to live a strong and happy life. I sincerely feel that anyone can benefit from the Buddha's teachings, regardless of their religion, way of life, or beliefs. In fact, it is okay to keep these things and just incorporate what is helpful from Buddhist teachings into your way of living. My particular Buddhist tradition, however, is not like the mindfulness movement that has become so popular in the West. Although mindfulness meditation, in which you repeatedly let go of thoughts, can be very helpful, in my tradition this is a beginner's practice known as *shamatha*, or calm abiding. This meditation, where you focus on something to anchor you in the moment, does induce relaxation and assists with attention, but it alone doesn't treat the root cause of a person's afflictions. Rather, the tradition of *lojong*, or mind training, treats what ails you. It not only tames your mind but trains you to think in a positive and healthy way. We use contemplative practices that build inner, mental strength, so that when we do encounter difficulties, we can easily endure them. This sort of analytic mind training is a path rather than a destination. It is meant to turn your mind toward your heart—toward kindness and compassion. Ultimately, it is a way of living that cultivates joy. This is what we call mind training. That is why it is not enough to simply work with your mind; you also are tasked to integrate what you learn into your everyday life.

The sole objective of this book is to wholeheartedly offer you wisdom that is at the core of my extensive education and give you ways in which you can benefit from these ancient teachings in a modern way. Each chapter in this book concludes with profound spiritual reflections and tried-and-true practices. After reading the reflection, take a moment to contemplate the story and then deeply ponder the correlating practice. Commit these practices to memory. Consider them as an arsenal of spiritual tools available for eliminating suffering. To reinforce these practices and to help you develop a wise mind and a kind heart, there is a mind training practice section at the end of this book. All of this is meant to be used in your day-to-day life. Although some practices may seem deceptively simple, I assure you that they are not. We tend to operate on habitual tendencies, and negative habits are not easily broken. That is why I urge you not to underestimate the power that training your mind can have in breaking these habits. Approach these practices with dogged determination. You will never know if these methods work if you don't apply them to your life. Try for at least several months, make a strong effort, and remember that everyone has the potential to become a happy buddha—even you.

# CHAPTER 1

# Nothing Lasts Forever

I SUSPECT you already know that nothing lasts forever. Take, for example, the global toilet paper shortage of 2020. Once the stay-at-home order was issued during the COVID-19 pandemic, fear triggered homebound people to get creative. So, they created the toilet paper-filled panic rooms of their dreams. These early shoppers mounded piles of toilet paper in their shopping carts, raced to the register, then rushed their stuffed vehicles home. They attempted to hoard their way to security, an effort to make toilet paper last forever. Seeing this, other shoppers raced to score what was left. Social media and funny memes swiftly emphasized this scarcity, which encouraged yet another wave of hoarding shoppers. When latecomers were faced with those empty store shelves, where toilet paper used to be, they were shocked! Believe it or not, many people thought that toilet paper would always be available. Empty-handed shoppers were left dumbfounded and muttering, "Why me?"

For decades I have enthusiastically acted as a spiritual and material support to students, communities, fellow monastics, and laypeople. Based on my many years of counseling troubled people, I've noticed that when something terrible happens to someone, the first question that most people seem to ask is, "Why me?" Of course, if something good happens in their life—for example, winning a million dollars in the lottery—they do not ask, "Why me?" Instead, they joyfully accept their good fortune and announce, "I am so lucky; I have lots of money to spend! I'm sure to be happy now!" That's the way we judge our circumstances. We're happy when things go our way and unhappy when they don't. But is it helpful to take the good and reject the bad? Life inevitably has both good and bad circumstances. Furthermore, asking "Why me?" does not help you resolve the problem. It is like asking, "Which comes first, the chicken or the egg?" You will never know the answer. So why ponder such questions? The next time you encounter something terrible, do not ask, "Why me?" Instead, ask yourself, "Which came first, the chicken or the egg?" Because both questions are equally ineffectual.

It's so easy to fall prey to the "why me" voice of self-pity in your head, but I implore you to instead accept the reality of the problem, just as it is. It's empowering to take accountability for the issues in your life. If you accept your dire circumstances, you can transform problematic matters and in turn apply suitable solutions. First, you must genuinely believe the fundamental truth of impermanence. You must understand that life is always changing and that nothing lasts forever. Not even toilet paper. However, simply hearing about the truth of change and having an intellectual understanding that nothing lasts forever is not enough. You must live your life as though nothing lasts forever. That is why part of this book's mission is to help free you of feeling stuck in your hardships and stuck with the useless question of "Why me?"

## A REASON FOR HOPE

It's important to muster up the courage and accept the reality of your life just as it unfolds. In truth, just being alive is a great adventure. You will have all sorts of good experiences, but you will also encounter some unwelcome surprises. Some surprises might even seem devastating. Still, one thing is certain: there is always hope because everything is temporary. You, and everything you encounter, are between a hello and a goodbye. Change is inevitable. The sooner you can accept this reality, the sooner you can stop asking "Why me?" and instead face your problems so you can find real solutions.

When we flesh out the cause of the toilet paper shortage, many of us become terrified of the immutable truth that nothing lasts forever. The truth is that everything is constantly changing. But another unwavering truth is that you are much more intelligent than your fears. Subconsciously, you know for a fact that change is valuable. For example, the pandemic lockdown of 2020 determined my food choices. Since my lockdown occurred in a monastery in Nepal, I was left eating whatever was in the communal pantry. We had simple foods like instant noodles or rice for every meal. My mind was grateful for the food, but my weary tastebuds tired of the same meals for months on end. A change couldn't come sooner! Fortunately, the lockdown did not last forever, so now I can genuinely appreciate a variety of foods. I will enjoy the variety while I can and will do so even more knowing that it is fleeting, like life itself. We should all feel so fortunate that things don't last forever. Can you imagine eating the same food forever? Would even your favorite food remain your favorite if you had to eat it forever? Imagine eating just cheese pizza, or my favorite, the plant-based Impossible Burger, forever! Fortunately, we live in a phenomenal world that is filled with change. Change, as well as the variety it brings, makes our mortal existence more enjoyable.

The rainbow is a symbol of hope. There would be no colorful rainbow if it weren't for the rain. You must weather the storm to even glimpse a rainbow. The weather is a perfect example of the variety and surprises your life holds. Surely you have noticed that lately this variety has been more varied than expected, with fire tornados, orange skies, raining ash, deep freezes in the desert, molten rock streams, tropical snow, as well as houses and cars floating downstream. This all sounds like the stuff of science fiction, but this is part of the dynamic, ever-changing world we are living in.

In mid-February 2021, in the United States, the typically temperate state of Texas plummeted into an unexpected and lengthy deep freeze. The electrical grid, household pipes, and water resources were no match for the polar vortex. Infrastructure failures left more than 4.5 million Texas homes without power and resulted in 246 deaths. The events in Texas were catastrophic, but like the rainbow, there was hope! The snow melted and the utilities returned, giving Texans a chance to acknowledge the problems they faced, repair the issues, and weatherize properly. Even though the calamity with the

Texas power grid will not be easily resolved, it brought awareness to a life-threatening problem so that helpful changes can be made. If you accept the reality of your troubles, change will help to change you. You have an incredible, natural ability to meet and adapt to the challenges of your life simply by accepting your problems and then evolving with the changes. You must take responsibility for your own world and rest your mind in the fact that no matter how great the storm, a colorful rainbow of hope awaits you.

Change provides surprises and diversity; just as no two faces are exactly the same, no two life experiences are the same. Furthermore, your face will change over time, and your life experience will alter, too. Transformation is inevitable—that is why the first part of taking charge of your life is adopting the understanding that life itself is subject to change. Life, without a doubt, will end in death. As a fact, you will pass away one day, as so many have before you. I urge you not to overly focus on the finality part, however, and instead focus on healthy ways to live so you can appreciate your life's journey right here and right now.

You need to be practical and know what is of benefit to your life so that when you are on your deathbed, you can say, "I had a happy life that was worth living." I can't stress the importance of this enough! Too many people waste their lives either depressed from clinging to unpleasant encounters in their past or anxiously pondering what might happen in the unforeseeable future. While it may not be apparent at first, both of these emotional dispositions are self-centered. Instead of thinking so much about yourself and your inevitable end, I invite you to consider the changing world around you. Nothing that is in your present experience will last forever. Not one object, not one feeling, not one circumstance, not your perception, and not even awareness will stay the same. But I assure you, reformation is your rainbow of hope. If you entirely accept the inevitability of change, you can undoubtedly endure the fleeting, painful parts of your life.

Believing that nothing lasts forever is one of those things that is easier said than done. Imagine you just purchased a brand-new smartphone or any other piece of current technology that you've had your eye on for some time. Furthermore, you have always wanted something state of the art like this, and now you finally have the money to purchase it. As you do for most new things, you quickly become overly attached to this gadget and its services. How would you feel if something unexpected happened to your brand-new gadget? How would you feel if the screen cracked, if it fell into water, or if it simply wouldn't fully charge? Even if something minor happens to it, you're more than likely to turn irritable and unhappy. But if you simply reminded yourself of the truth that nothing lasts forever, you would not get so agitated when something like this happens. You would understand that it is natural for things to alter over time. When you contemplate the reality of change, your mind will begin to expect it, and you won't feel as surprised. As a result, you'll be far more relaxed when something breaks or gets lost.

Perhaps you're okay with things around you changing. Maybe you don't feel so invested in your gadgets. But are you all right with the changes you see in the mirror? Are you okay when there is a change in your health, your pain level, or your mobility? Some people are heavily attached to their bodies and have a tough time enduring the unavoidable changes it undergoes over the years. When you are too attached to your body, you tend to have a corresponding notion that your body is the same as it was in the past and has remained unchanged over time. Sometimes this leads to taking up an age-inappropriate manner of dress and behavior. But frankly, neither youthful clothing nor behavior can stop the aging process—only perhaps disguise it a little.

If you're fortunate to live a long life, it's just a matter of time before a stranger offers you a senior discount. Someone might point out that they are grandparents, too, or simply mention that your hair is a little more salt than pepper. If you are attached to your age and someone merely hints at the fact that you are growing old, that alone could be enough to make you consider plastic surgery. Seeing your body age may make you quite upset. Age-attached persons refuse to acknowledge the truth of just how much their bodies have changed.

If you are age-attached, it may be challenging for you, but it's in your best interest to accept the reality of how old you are. After all, only things like cheese improve with age. As your body becomes fragile over time, it needs even more excellent care. Accepting your age, respecting your limitations, and caring for your aging body is an act of kindness toward yourself and your loved ones.

Acceptance of the truth is critical to the development of joy! How can you feel happy if you're stuck in a web of lies? From this point forward, I encourage you to accept the truth of the temporary nature of things, including the hardships that you may encounter in life. When you are in the thick of your troubles, don't make matters worse for yourself by struggling with the truth. Accept your circumstances and cease to believe that the hardships, and the suffering these troubles cause, are indefinite. Don't cave in to your worries. Your incessant worrying results in deceptive mental fables, negative inner dialogue, and even greater suffering. If you feel trapped in your troubles, the practice at the end of this chapter can help you.

## THE CLOUDS OF EMOTION

I have observed that those suffering from a bout of depression are especially prone to assuming that their hardships and sufferings are hopelessly permanent. Even mild depression has an obscuring quality that makes it even harder to accept the truth of change. It makes you feel like you'll never be free from whatever troubles you encounter, so it takes more effort to see the fleeting nature of hardship. But I have a strong wish for those of you who feel stuck in your depression: please rest assured that improvement is a certainty! Hope is a solid reality. Although they may seem permanent to you, these hopeless feelings of insecurity and sadness are like temporary clouds in the sky. While these clouds of emotion obscure the sun, the truth of change, it still shines brightly behind. Your difficulties needn't feel permanent. When you feel emotionally stuck, committing to a strong practice of contemplating impermanence can help lift your mind from the clouds of sadness. As a word of caution, if after such a practice you still feel hopelessly entrenched in depression, please accept the reality of the problem by seeking appropriate professional care. Clinical depression is a serious medical matter that can be addressed with the right treatment. Once under treatment, ask your physician if this sort of practice is advisable.

Please keep in mind that change is inevitable. You needn't feel trapped in negative emotions, regardless of how awful existence seems, because nothing is permanent. You can take charge of the improvements you wish to see. If you accept reality just as it is, you will encourage your mind to seek realistic alternatives. Focus on the inevitability of change and be extra kind to yourself. Any problem you face and the resulting hurt that you feel, no matter how strong, will pass as surely as clouds part and the sun shines again.

## BECOMING FAMILIAR WITH LIFE'S UNPREDICTABILITY

The COVID-19 pandemic provided an excellent lesson in the reality that nothing lasts forever. People across the globe lost economic stability, job security, support services, lifestyle norms, and even some measure of hope. They also lost good mental and physical health. But most significantly, people lost their lives. This fateful event showed our shared mortality and how well we humans react to significant changes. Many were left asking, "Why me?" But others courageously faced the truth and sought out a solution to this world-changing crisis. Once the Centers for Disease Control and Prevention and the World Health Organization brought to light the catastrophic nature of this contagion, various collaborative efforts developed between different sectors of society. Private pharmaceutical firms joined forces with public health agencies and university laboratories to combat the growing number of COVID casualties. After fervent attempts to develop a cure, helpful vaccines were ultimately generated widely enough to slow down the speed with which this infectious disease was able to claim lives. The acknowledgment of the truth of change by medical and scientific researchers was instrumental in helping reduce the enormous amount of suffering caused by this widespread ailment. This exemplifies how accepting the truth is the real key to positive transformation.

In my corner of the world, we had to accept a different truth. In the West, vaccines were as easy to come by as a Coca-Cola. But where I live, the COVID vaccine was as precious and rare as gold. I was fortunate enough to be offered a vaccine shortly after they were developed, but I refused it—not because I am against vaccines, but because I knew that at that critical time, one other person would be denied a life-saving shot if I accepted it. My life's work has enabled me a level of comfort and familiarity with life's unpredictability. As a result, I am not afraid of death. I am certain that death, like every-thing else, also doesn't last forever.

I am an enormous fan of the prominent psychiatrist Dr. Ian Steven-son and his fascinating, meticulous studies of children's memories of their former lives. Dr. Stevenson went to great lengths to scientifically investigate the details of his findings as a researcher at the University of Virginia. What he discovered was enough to turn even a hardcore skeptic into a believer in the concept of rebirth. Dr. Stevenson stud-ied thousands of children's past-life recollections from around the world. Time and time again, he could locate prominent figures from their memories and validate that these children's past-life memories were highly accurate. I can relate to his findings given that I also have an identifiable previous life. Consequently, I know that death, like everything else, is simply a natural process of transformation and change. Some people find this hard to believe. However, just a basic understanding of your forever-changing existence can make a huge difference in the quality of your life and encourage positive ways of living.

Suppose you accept the truth that nothing lasts forever. In that case, you also know that no single stage of any individual process will last forever either, including the process of dying. That is part of the reason I don't fear death. I am aware that there is a myriad of ideas about what happens after death, but I'd like to share what I have learned on the subject. I don't wish to frighten you; I merely intend to be helpful and familiarize you with what I have discovered about this process. I hope that imparting the knowledge that I possess on the subject will help eliminate some of your fear of one of the most mysterious and most significant changes of all.

People avoid the topic of their mortality because the idea of it can be frightening. There is nothing to fear, though; dying is as natural as life itself. And if you've read any of Dr. Stevenson's books, as I have, then it's logical to assume that death is just a steppingstone to a new life. You needn't believe what I say; after all, it's wise to do your own research on the subject. But I hope you will consider the knowledge I've gleaned from a lifetime of profound study of the works that have been passed down and verified by practitioners over many centuries. First, I would like to give you a basic breakdown of the changes you'll undergo during the dying process to make it very predictable. The more you know, the less surprised you will be when your own time comes.

### The dying process

Your body is made of four general elements: The earth element, like the minerals that make up your bones; the water element, like your blood; the fire element, like the warmth of your body; and the air element, like the breath in your lungs. When your body has nearly reached its end, your intelligent mind—or soul, essence, or whatever you want to call it—knows it is time to let go.

At first, your body and your mind begin to separate, causing a series of physical changes. Initially, the earth element will leave your body, which gives rise to a feeling of your body falling, even though clearly it is not. Next, the water element leaves your body, causing thirst and a sense of dryness. Then the fire element departs, causing your body temperature to gradually cool. Then, lastly, the wind element leaves your body, and your breathing rattles, then stops. These are universal *natural* stages of death that any hospice care workers would encounter—obviously, these are not the stages of a sudden or drug-induced death. It's essential for you to be kind and gentle with yourself as you go through this process. Once breath stops and your heart ceases to beat, from the perspective of medical science, this is the moment of your body's clinical death. This is all quite natural; everybody'must go through it, and it's simply another change. If this is too much for your mind to handle at this time, try to imagine the state you'd be in if you lived indefinitely. In middle age, one's body already feels a little achy. Can you imagine how achy you'd feel in a hundred more years?

Once clinical death is established and the body's organs begin to shut down, you will behold a white light. Seeing this light is like seeing something in a lucid dream. In a lucid dream, you are aware that you are dreaming and thus feel a sense of control over what you encounter. You needn't fear anything in this type of dream. According to the Hospice Organization of America, this period of sensory change may begin just prior to clinical death. The dying person may experience and vocalize hallucinations that they encounter. They may hear, see, or feel things that the living do not sense. These hallucinations may be frightening or comforting to the dying person, depending on their content. The person may speak of seeing religious figures. The dying person may talk about taking a trip or other activities related to travel, like packing a bag or boarding an airplane. The awareness of their death may bring a peaceful feeling, particularly if it carries the prospect of reunification with loved ones or with spiritual beings. As you progress through this stage, either before or after clinical death, please know that even if you encounter a fearsome beast, it is not real and is merely a projection of your extraordinary mind. In fact, if you understand this, you might as well enjoy any apparitions within this lucid dream-like state. At this point, your mind is fully letting go of your body.

After the period of sensory changes and the appearance of the white light, there follows a red light and then blackness. These appearances are enough to recognize with certainty that one is experiencing the dying process. This experience is like falling asleep. Our ordinary perceptions, such as hearing and seeing, subside. We gradually enter a very subtle state of consciousness, followed by the actual, deep tranquil state where ordinary sensory perception ceases. When we encounter blackness, we cannot perceive anything; this is like fainting. The remarkable thing about being unconscious is it is quite restful.

After this state of blackness, we see clear light. The clear light is the most direct encounter you can have with your true nature, or what I call buddha nature. The experience of clear light is accompanied by a very distinctive spacious, free, empty feeling. Some Buddhist practices, such as familiarization with impermanence and the stages of death, offer preparation for this encounter. Once you encounter the clear light, my tradition states that you are officially deceased. Because meditation on the clear light provides the greatest opportunity for enlightenment, it is imperative to pay close attention and remain wholly focused on what you are experiencing. The clear light lasts from a single moment up to three days and can result in awakening. It is a spiritual experience of an enormous empty space. There are no sensory objects or pretty colors, just the vast emptiness of the clear light vision. This clean, pure state of being, free of hallucinations, can give way to mental projections. Remember, whatever you encounter, you needn't fear; it is merely a product of your mind, similar to a hallucination. Because of this, we should establish healthy habits in our lives now. Those healthy habits—for example, of meditation, prayer, generosity, self-reflection, and actively using the practices in this book—can help you deal with your mental state throughout the dying process. In my tradition of Buddhism, we believe that how you live your current life, and your state of mind at the time of death, influences your future life. Our spiritual practices aim to eliminate fears and regrets so that we can live and die in peace, joy, and possibly even bliss. The better your practice, the better your outcome.

## PREPARING FOR THE FUTURE

Your strong karmic impressions and habitual tendencies play a significant part in determining your future. These imprints tend to carry over from one life to the next. Dr. Ian Stevenson's research of children's past-life memories touches on this phenomenon. He found correlations between the recollection of how one died in a past life and current phobias. For example, if a child had a past-life memory of drowning, they exhibited an intense fear of water in their current life. He noted that children lose their phobic behaviors once their recollection of that previous life fades. Dr. Stevenson also collected many cases of children who possessed birth defects and birthmarks associated with fatal wounds from their previous lives. Apparently, past-life experiences not only affect a person's current life mentally but also physically. How one lives, how one dies, and one's mental state at the time of death are all important factors in rebirth. Knowledge of our impermanence and mind training practices can help you prepare for the colossal change called death.

As a reincarnated Buddhist master, I am a firm believer in rebirth. I have returned to assist beings in awakening to their true nature. For me to help you, however, you needn't believe in the possibility of living multiple lives. In fact, whether you chose a religious preference or not doesn't matter to me. What is most essential is for you to focus on the best and healthiest way to live your life now. Your life does not last forever and that makes it all the more precious. In my tradition, we live our lives moment by moment, and consistently mindful of death. We have a certain meditation on death that focuses on the following, which you can take a moment to reflect on too.

> *Death is certain. You can't escape death, so you must practice now in order to reach your highest spiritual and mental potential. The time of death is uncertain. Your physical body is vulnerable to disease and life-threatening situations. It doesn't matter whether you are young or old, sick or well—you can die regardless of such circumstances. Life is the dash between birth and death. You don't know how long that dash will be, so practice now, not later. Your spiritual and mental practice is the only thing that will help you at your time of death. Your wealth, relatives, friends, body, and the like can't help you at the time of your death. Thinking in this way*

*may seem morbid, but it makes your life more meaningful, helps you focus on what is truly important, and lets you face death with courage and hope.*

The main point of this meditation is to accept change and live with the thought that you and those around you will not be around forever. It's imperative to not spend your life worried, upset, or in meaningless squabbles, but instead make your fleeting existence as extraordinary as possible.

To drive the point home, imagine that you are one of five prisoners. All five of you have hurt one another and consequently are mutual enemies. To your dismay, you are all placed in a small holding cell together. After being forced to be in the company of those you despise, you are then told that all five of you will be executed the next day. At first you may argue, but once it truly dawns on you that everyone's lives end tomorrow, do you sincerely think you'd squabble throughout the night? If you offered forgiveness and were kind to your fellow inmates, how would that change things for you?

This situation is no different than our real lives. Right now, we are living together in this dynamic, changing world. We all rely on one another for things like goods and services, yet we are all prone to arguing and self-focused "why me" thinking. Thirty, forty, fifty years from now, you may be gone. Perhaps even sooner—who knows? Possibly fifteen years from now. It could be even shorter than that, maybe just a few days. Nothing lasts forever, so why waste your valuable fleeting life fighting with others and being upset? You are worthy of a life of joy, but it truly is up to you to make that happen.

This reminds me of a story. There once was a man who really wanted to go to heaven. He was spiritually strict; he avoided the corrupting influence of the world by living bare naked in the woods and eating only one small meal a day for many years. As a result, his health began to fail. When he finally went to see a doctor, he was fragile, shaky, and covered in insect bites. The doctor examined this sickly man and told him that he needed to take better care of his health or else he'd meet an untimely demise. After some consideration, the doctor took pity on his wayward patient. He offered the man a free month at a superb health resort in Switzerland. He hoped the man would recuperate before resuming what the doctor wished would be a healthier spiritual practice.

The man objected because he was deeply committed to his spiritual practice of asceticism and could never stay in such a luxurious resort. But the doctor spelled it out in black and white for him by saying, "The choice is up to you: Switzerland or heaven." A few minutes after leaving the hospital, the man shakily came running back into the doctor's office, exclaiming, "Okay, okay! I've decided—I'll take Switzerland!" This is human nature: what we want the most is the contentment of happiness, and we want it in this life rather than in some afterlife. It's best to be realistic. The reality is that nothing lasts forever; things change, so why not be in charge of how they change?

## RIPPLES IN THE POND

The reality of change is proof that your life is miraculously moldable. Your life is like water, which has no shape of its own. If you pour water into a round container, it takes on a round shape; if you pour it into a square container, it takes on a square shape. By the same token, your life takes the form of your choices. Good choices lead to good outcomes. Bad choices lead to bad outcomes. Many people are making the good choice to meditate to calm their minds. Making the choice to work with your mind is a step in the right direction. But for lasting joy, it is not enough to simply calm your mind; you must also choose to be an architect and work with your mind in such a way that you build a world worth living in. Furthermore, you mustn't work only with your mind, but also with your heart! Your mind and heart operate as a team. If you make wise choices that include caring for and sharing with others, you'll create a world filled with peace and compassion. Your choices generate change.

Have you ever tossed a rock into a pond and watched its ripples grow bigger and wider until they reach the shore? It's incredible how such a small action can make such a significant effect! The decisions you make and the behavior you choose to adopt have a similar effect: each starts small, then builds momentum. For example, if one of your fellow employees is acting intolerably miserable, their bad mood tends to spread like an infectious ailment. It ripples throughout the entire workplace until everyone is infected with their contagious irritability. Everyone is so grumpy they can't wait for the workday to end. Conversely, suppose someone at work is especially happy. They are smiling, waving, and generally friendly to others. In that case, their cheerfulness has the potential to ripple throughout the entire workplace, like a catchy song.

Many people assume that their choices and way of acting merely affect those closest to them, but that is a grave mistake. When you consider the effect that those closest to you have on the people around them, and the impact those people have on others, you can see that the circle of influence keeps widening. Your choices have an effect that is so far-reaching you could not possibly know just what the implication of your actions will be. Then, after the effects of your decision make their rounds through others, it affects you again, in something like a feedback loop. It is much like how waves hit the shore then return to their source through the undertow. What we call karma are the effects of what you have circulated returning to you. That is why a happy world starts with you. First, you need to make yourself happy. This begins with facing the reality of change and in particular the inevitable change we call death. You must understand the way things truly are, which this book can help you with.

I sincerely hope you choose to live strong mentally and have a happy heart. Don't waste this fleeting opportunity called life fussing over problems and inconveniences, over empty store shelves where toilet paper used to be. Don't simply ask, "Why me?" If you find yourself troubled by existence and are profoundly suffering, please remember whatever the problem is, it won't last. Nothing lasts forever; it is always in the process of changing, just like you. When you burn a log, does it disappear, or does it change into ash and smoke? Constant change is our shared reality. Take full advantage of this fact and be determined to be the architect of your ever-evolving world.

# Reflection

A long time ago, there was a powerful ruler who sought wisdom. He wondered how to make a sad man happy and a happy man sad. Since he didn't know where to begin, he asked his trusted spiritual advisor to help him find an answer. The holy man was confident he could find helpful feedback to such a wise question, so he wasted no time. He searched far and wide, but no one could give him an answer. With nowhere left to search, he decided to check the kingdom's run-down neighborhoods. After searching nearly every inch of the kingdom, he decided he might have to give up. It was then he heard some cheerful whistling. Following the chipper sound, he made his way down a dirt alley where a happy craftsman whistled away. "Hello, joyful merchant," the holy man greeted him. "Could you help me solve the problem of how to make a sad man happy and a happy man sad?" The tradesman thought for a moment, then insisted that he could provide him with a solution to his problem. A joyful expression spread across the advisor's face.

After a little more thought, the craftsman whispered something into the ear of his grandfather, who was assisting him in his work. The older man shuffled slowly into his workshop. After some banging, he returned carrying a shiny golden ring, which he handed to the holy man. "This is the solution?" the king's advisor said, not expecting a ring. He examined the jewelry closely. Suddenly, a broad grin spread on his face. "Oh yes! This will do!" Without hesitation, he gave the tradesman a bag of coins and then hastily made his way to the king. He couldn't wait to present him with the solution.

Once inside the palace gates, he rushed up the stairs and into the king's quarters. "Here is your answer, sire." The king looked miffed. He hadn't expected jewelry. The curious ruler carefully lifted the ring and examined it. After thorough analysis and contemplation, he stood there dumbfounded. "I see!" He beamed. He never thought that his spiritual advisor would bring him a ring that would cause him to reflect on time and change, on the past, present, and future. On the outside, the ring looked plain. But on the inside of the ring was inscribed the words, "This too shall pass."

Take the time to sit with these words: "This too shall pass." Indeed, like toilet paper, nothing lasts forever. Everything is changing. This reality, that you can't attach to anything, is easy to hear but difficult to internalize. Change can be painful. If you are experiencing pain, letting go of it feels pleasurable. Although like an itch that temporarily goes away after you scratch, the satisfaction you feel is only brief because the itchy feeling will return. Pain and pleasure are inevitable parts of life. You may be motivated to let go of pain because it hurts, but isn't the fleeting nature of pleasant experiences also painful? Having to let go of something or someone you enjoy induces pain. Pleasure and pain are as brief as your life.

Newborns have yet to learn much about life as we know it, but they have basic survival instincts, such as crying when they are hungry or sick. Over time, your experiences condition you to be a certain way beyond these instinctual drives. The Buddha said *all conditioned things have the nature of impermanence.* You may know this from your own childhood, but when you're young, your expiration date feels far away, so you aren't concerned about your mortality. But as you age, you see the finish line more clearly. Thoughts of your death can induce a terror—after all, it is your most significant change of all. That is why it is crucial to realize the inevitability of transformation.

Contemplating the fleeting, dynamic nature of things helps you generate intelligence and acceptance about how things genuinely are, so you don't get upset when faced with the reality of change and impermanence. When you think about people or encounter objects, you don't usually consider that they are in the process of alteration. You grasp at or attach to things, thinking they're unchanging and permanent. When you regularly reflect on things as being momentary, how your world appears to you will change. If you then wonder why it changes, you will find that there are different reasons. Change is dependent on causes and conditions. Your practice is to cultivate an awareness of how whatever you encounter is changing. Once you start accepting things as impermanent, you can begin to live your life and make decisions based on that truth. Spend twenty minutes mentally investigating the impermanence of life and the varied reasons, or causes and conditions, that are influencing such changes. Start with yourself; then consider those closest to you; then neighbors; then those that you feel indifferent toward; then your so-called enemies; and lastly, consider the impermanence of all beings. You cannot alter the reality that nothing lasts forever, but you can modify your reaction once you have a grounded understanding of the true nature of phenomena. From this point on, keep mindfully aware that nothing lasts forever.

# CHAPTER 2

# A Bad Case of GAS

I WOULD LIKE to address something that we all get on occasion and really stinks: GAS! I don't mean flatulence or a fart. I mean something that stinks much worse: greed, anger, and stupidity—or GAS, the acronym that Buddhist author, teacher, and scholar Dr. Kenneth K. Tanaka cleverly coined. This does not mean that gassiness and GAS don't have an obvious similarity. Both feel uncomfortable and can displease the people around you, but GAS is also the root of many disturbing emotions and leads to unhappiness. It is especially insidious where consumerism is concerned. Consumerism has the word *consume* in it for a good reason; the theory implies that increasing one's appetite for purchasing goods and services benefits the economy. But consumerism has generated a lot of hungry people, and with all that consumption, it is no wonder everyone seems plagued by GAS.

## G IS FOR GREED

A perfect example of this is the infamous Black Friday. This sales event truly lives up to its dark history. While many myths surround the origin of the day, the term was coined in the 1950s by police officers in the city of Philadelphia. Law enforcement had to spend long hours on that frantic Friday managing mobs of unruly shoppers and shoplifters on the first shopping day of the Christmas season, as well as enthused sports fanatics in town for the immensely popular annual Army-Navy football game. As a shopping event, it gradually took root across the United States and conveniently fell on the day after the U.S. holiday of Thanksgiving, when many shoppers had time off work to shop for Christmas gifts. Over time, Black Friday changed from a bustling shopping day into a riotous conquest for affordable goods. It can sometimes be as perilous as Spain's Running of the Bulls. The quintessential Black Friday scenario begins with long lines of early shoppers erecting campsites at a large retail super-store or mall overnight. They hope to get their hands on the few big deals the stores advertise to attract shoppers—typically, just a few big-ticket items that have been steeply discounted. Still, the shoppers wait and wait, then once the door opens, a mob recklessly makes a dash for the sale items—everyone pushing, shoving, and racing one another as if bulls were chasing them! Once they get their hands on one of these deals, a fight might ensue as others grab for it. Some-times it comes to mere blows, while other times, the altercation can be life-threatening.

Black Friday has taken root in other countries and has expanded into other sales events like Cyber Monday. If only the little-known "Giving Tuesday" were more widely adopted! Whether in person or online, it's clear that shopping is a popular pastime. It's not entirely your fault that you like to shop. Your brain's reward system activates when you purchase items, especially when you get a deal. This creates a feeling so powerful and pleasant that it's easy to forget rationality and spend money with reckless abandon. MRI scans confirm that the effects of shopping on brain activity are similar to the pleasant feel-ing produced by drugs—and shopping too is addictive. It can also in turn generate greed. Don't get me wrong, I am not wholly opposed to purchasing or possessing things. You needn't turn your back on modern life and give up all your possessions. I only hope you take a good look and consider how greed, the G in GAS, can negatively affect your peace and happiness.

Most everyone living in our modern world values material com-forts. People delight in luxuriously furnished homes; the latest, greatest automobile; and the most up-to-date technology. This fond-ness for things is much like a monkey trap. In Asia, there is a simple method used to trap a monkey: all you need to do is carve a small hole in a hollow gourd or coconut, put a nut inside of it, and then tie it to a tree. Once the monkey discovers the nut, it will reach through the small opening to get it, but when it tries to pull its full fist out, its hand no longer fits through the hole. The monkey refuses to let go of the delicious nut inside despite struggling to get free. All the monkey has to do is let go of the nut, but it stays trapped because of its fondness for nuts. In a similar way, you may not recognize the adverse side effects of your fondness for, and attachment to, newer and better things. I would like you to consider in what ways your dreams and desires may ensnare you like a monkey trap.

There is an old story about greed and its adverse side effects that I'd like to tell you. Once upon a time, there was a starving peasant. He was hungry because he didn't have any land to farm on. He knew his king had vast farmland holdings, so one fateful day he plucked up the courage to ask the king for some farmland. The king was clever, however, and saw the man had an extreme desire for land, beyond what he needed for his own sustenance. So, after mulling it over a bit, the wise king offered the hungry peasant every foot of land he could walk on in a day, from the spot the peasant stood outward. There was a catch, though; he had to reverse his steps and be back at that exact spot by sundown. The hungry peasant profusely thanked the wise king and waited with bated breath in anticipation for the sun to come up.

The peasant excitedly returned to the spot at sunrise and began his trek outward. He walked and walked; for miles, he walked. Occasionally he'd stop and marvel over how much land he'd stepped foot on. He looked back toward the spot he started from and thought, "This is more than enough farmland; I could have enough food for me and enough to sell for a profit!" He really liked the idea of making a profit. Hence, he continued to walk outward, dreaming of his profit and ignoring the position of the sun. By afternoon, he was dead exhausted. He had walked so far out that his feet burned with pain and his body ached with exhaustion. He had to sit down and rest a while but then noticed that the sun's position had drastically changed; it was close to sundown! Recalling the king's condition, the hungry peasant panicked. He jumped to his feet, turned around, and ran as fast as his weary body could carry him toward the spot where he had started.

Because he was too busy daydreaming of all the land he would amass, he hadn't realized how far he had walked! He tried to make it back quickly, but the sun was nearly down and he was consumed by exhaustion. There was no way he'd return in time. The peasant fell into a heap of disappointment and defeat. He slowly shuffled away from the smart king's land with exactly as much as he'd had the previous day: which was nothing!

This is one example of how the hunger for possessions, how greed, can blind us. It's normal to have dreams and desires, but please always remember that you can't possibly have it all! Besides, what you are really dreaming of and desiring is a life of inner peace and joy, not just a life with all the goods and services you could hope for.

I heard that the word that people use the most in their lives is the word "I." "I" listen for "I" a lot! "I" listen to it so frequently that "I" am amazed by the amount "I" hear the word "I"! It is incredible how much you'll find the word when you're looking for it. Attachment is *not* just about things; it's mainly about your self-focus and your effort to make yourself happy. This is exemplified through the social science theory called the tragedy of the commons. This theory claims that anyone with access to a commonly shared resource ends up acting in their own self-interest and, by doing so, depletes the resource for all. For example, an overconsumption of coffee has led to the depletion of certain coffee plants. Overfishing has led to the depletion of certain fish, like tuna, and overuse of groundwater has led to droughts. The desire to consume is self-motivated, regardless of any negative consequences it has on the world as a whole.

Consumerism uses your self-absorption to its advantage. It sells you products and services with the promise they will make your life better. Its tactics know no bounds because desires are rooted in self-attachment and are ever-present, unless and until you choose to roll up your sleeves and do what it takes to overcome them. Until then, you are on the hunt for satisfaction. Not just for storefront items, but for what other people have, too! You want what the smiling and laughing people in the ads have so you can be happy like they are. You suspect that other people, whether in advertisements or in real life, have something better than you. You compare your stuff with other people's things, and this breeds feelings of greed, competitiveness, and jealousy. Societies seem set up this way; even the letter grading system is such that an "A" means you're excellent and an "F" means you've failed. Parents tell their kids they have to do well in school. Doing well to a child means they must do excellent work, be an "A" student, and compete with their classmates for the top spot. Encouraging such competition from childhood in this way has its advantages and disadvantages. .

Competition fuels progress and improvements in society, but, on the other hand, it causes so much jealousy and division among people. Consumerism capitalizes on this desire to "keep up with the Joneses," so to speak. For instance, once I went to buy a new pair of glasses and felt pressured to compete. The sales assistant kept trying to persuade me to get trendy and in-style glasses even though I preferred simple glasses. He said, "Everyone is wearing these frames nowadays, not those out-of-date frames." I didn't cave into the pressure even though he seemed determined to make me a carbon copy of other visually challenged people. It's this type of pressure that causes you to feel inadequate and suffer from jealousy.

I want to encourage you to take a step back and ask yourself what you really want from your life. Do you want material objects over happiness? It seems as though the resounding answer to that question is yes. In the Pacific Ocean, there is a massive patch of plastic garbage that has accumulated over decades and has caused considerable damage to the ocean and the creatures that inhabit it. It's hard to know who is responsible for this massive garbage mound since it's so far from any country's shore. Still, it clearly represents how the world's desire for material things has gotten out of hand. This is one of the reasons why I buy things secondhand. You have a choice: You can be content with what you have, or you can continue to hunger for things outside of yourself. Do you choose the paradise of contentment or the manufactured happiness of a plastic island?

This choice reminds me of a parable. Once there was a mother with three children, and one day they asked her for some oranges. She didn't have any, but she did have some lemons, so she gave them those instead. The first child picked up one of the lemons and protested: "Yuck, a sour lemon! I wanted a sweet orange." The second child simply ate one of the lemons and sulked: "This is not an orange." The third child wasn't attached to the idea of getting an orange; she appreciated receiving a lemon. Accepting the truth, she happily squeezed out the juice, added some delicious honey, and shared a refreshing glass of lemonade with her family. Everyone was happy! When life gives you lemons—as the saying goes—make lemonade! It's up to you to choose which of these three children you want to be like. You can decide to make a big fuss when you don't get what you want, grudgingly bear the sour taste of disappointment, or be content with what you do have and make something delicious from it to share with others.

## A Is for Anger

The greed-induced Black Friday shopping frenzies have a history of turning into chaotic mobbing. The growth of consumerism has led to some extreme violence on that day. Pushing, fighting, stabbings, and shootings among Black Friday holiday shoppers have all been reported in various locations across the globe! Such anger may seem wise at the time because you feel it will protect or help you. Yet it really is very harmful and even interferes with rational thinking. Simply put, this level of anger clouds your mind then impairs your good judgment.

Anger—the A in GAS—is merely a response to something that we find unfair or threatening. But did you know that it is a learned response? People react to unfair or dire situations in diverse ways. Some people cry, some shout, and some take it out on other people around them. It really depends on what you've learned. I once met a young boy who asked me for help with his conditioned anger issues. He told me that his anger started after he shouted at a classmate and, in doing so, silenced his entire class. Since then, he has thought of anger as a handy tool that gave him power. Because of this, he used his anger frequently when things seemed unfair or threatening. But as a result, his anger became uncontrollable and interfered with his close relationships.

I taught him some practices that would help him develop compassion to quell his anger. I told him that compassion and love are great antidotes to anger. For example, you can envision the target of your anger as your mom, or any other figure, who loves you unconditionally but is only human and so makes mistakes. If you believe in rebirth, then who knows—perhaps they actually *were* your mom in a past life. I taught this practice to him and, because he seemed like an ambitious young man, I further suggested that he consider all conscious beings as a dear mother. Then three months later, he returned. He arrived late in the day, and so he had to go straight to the monastery's guest house for the night. It was hot in the guest house, so he opened the windows to get a cool breeze. In the morning, I visited him and asked him how he slept. He said, "Just horribly! It was very hot, and there were tons of little bugs buzzing around my ears all night and mosquitos trying to bite me. I followed your guidelines though and didn't harm one conscious being. How could I possibly hurt all those moms!" This shows you that a little guidance, some ambition, and some gratitude for a loving being goes a long way. Even longer if you set a goal and apply good old-fashioned determination. With some effort you can begin to unlearn any negative learned behaviors and habits. Indeed, with all the aggression that the day causes, perhaps stores should offer anger management classes on Black Friday instead of deals.

Anger is the sort of destructive emotion that directly harms us and those around us. For example, social media can generally be used as a helpful resource, but unfortunately, this online craze has developed a downside. Once again, let's use the theory of the tragedy of the commons as a means to understand the internet as a common, corruptible resource. Since it is available to all individuals, people tend to use it for their self-centered interests. People air their dirty laundry, so to speak, by expressing their negative thoughts and opinions to the detriment of others. They write unkind, self-righteous, and even cruel comments to troll or provoke others for entertainment.

Furthermore, because reviews and opinions can be anonymous, there needn't be any accountability for unhinged commenting. Anyone can broadcast some angry opinion or thought instantly for all the world to read, whether it is true or not. Many of these comments can remain readable for some indefinite amount of time. When you consider the ripple effect, these negative words could affect more people than you will ever know.

Feeling perturbed is normal; however, if you've developed a persistent, quick temper at the slightest disturbance, you're out of touch with reality. When things don't go your way, you twist and warp your impression of something, or someone, in order to justify your anger. Distorting your perception in this way can develop into a bad habit. For example, if someone offers you constructive criticism, you immediately get offended and consider the person who uttered the unsavory remark as a hurtful individual and nothing else. The problem with this is you can't accept the truth. That's why it is important to challenge your anger. If you deeply consider your anger, you'll see various contributing factors at play. However, these aspects are distorted by your rage. You only see one part contributing to your anger: the person, or thing, that made you feel on edge. Having someone or something to blame makes your upset seem solid and real.

For instance, imagine someone riding your tail while driving. They repeatedly honk their horn because they think you are moving too slow. You are going the speed limit, so you get angry at that person. But what you don't consider is that you are a little hungry, so you already feel irritable. You don't need to be anywhere on time, but they may be late for work. They can't be late—if they are late, they could get fired. They have a family to provide for, and they are sick with the flu on top of it.

There are always multiple reasons why people behave the way they do. Once, I was going for a walk and passed a bar. As I passed by, a drunk man inside shouted very loudly for me to join him. As a monk, I could not go to a bar, so I ignored him and continued to walk. When I did this, the man got furious. He left the bar and followed after me, irritably asking why I didn't join him. At first, I avoided him, assuming he could see that I was a monk and knew that monks don't drink alcohol. But then I recalled that there are hidden factors that could have incited his anger. He may not have known that monks cannot enter a bar, he may have been very intoxicated, he might have felt rejected. Rather than take his anger personally or run away, I put my palms together and said to him very sincerely and politely, "I'm sorry." As soon as I did this, the man immediately became calmer.

You needn't succumb to feeling upset. When you encounter anger, either another's anger directed at you or your own anger directed at others, be smart. Consider all the possible variables. When you examine the causes of such behavior, you'll respond in a more healthy and mature way.

## S Is for Stupidity

When you don't consider all the factors involved, you suffer from a form of ignorance, or, to make the acronym work, stupidity—the S in GAS. The cause of both greed and anger is ignorance of the way things truly are. There are various things you can be ignorant about, but being stupid about yourself is one of the most problematic. Being stupid about yourself is not a reflection of your level of education; I mean being ignorant of how you exist in this world. There is a concept in Buddhism called no self. This concept does not mean that you don't exist or that there isn't a self; you exist and will continue to exist. It means that you'll undergo so many changes that you will not stay the same you. For example, the five-year-old you was a lot different than you are now. Another thing to consider about yourself is that you only exist because of everything around you that supports your existence. You rely on everything around you to live in an ideal way, and the awareness of this should ensure your indebtedness to this world. Unfortunately, it is not the case that most people have such an awareness. The vast majority of the eight billion human beings on our planet remain ignorant to their reliance on everything and everyone in this vast universe. As a result, people live solely for their own benefit. Those who aren't living solely for themselves are the notable people who stick in your mind, like the Dalai Lama, Mother Teresa, or Martin Luther King, Jr. In one way or another, they are mostly those who help our world and are engaged in some altruistic, philanthropic, or humanitarian work. This illuminates the fact that you lead a meaningful life when you think of benefiting what is around you, not just yourself.

Even though you live among so many other people, do you find yourself mostly thinking about yourself? If I were to ask you to tell me your problems, would you easily talk on and on about them? Most people find it easy to recount their own problems but disregard the difficulties that a family member or friend is going through. Would you need a few minutes to produce some examples of their problems? How can you know, care for, or be close to anyone if you don't know what they are going through? If it's easy for you to discuss your own issues but difficult for you to drum up problems that your friends or family face, you may be overly preoccupied with yourself. Being this self-centered is like driving sightless, like that old cartoon character Mr. Magoo. You're driving around, you think you're doing a fine job; however, you can't see things clearly, so you're driving off the road, endangering the world around you.

Self-centered stupidity is another way of saying that you get in the way of yourself. You are your own obstacle to happiness, and you aren't always aware of that. I do not mean that your life is not valuable or that you shouldn't take good care of yourself. In fact, it is highly beneficial for you to enthusiastically think, "I would like to be happy!" We get in the way of ourselves when we overly focus on our own happiness or become self-cherishing. Self-cherishing is the mind that regards oneself as being more important than others. One easy way to detect this mind is by looking at a group photo with you in it. Who is the first person you look at in the picture? Most of us look at ourselves! We are very self-focused.

I know that I've had my moments of self-cherishing. Many years back, when I was a young boy, my mom suggested that we go for a walk and get some fresh air. We discussed it for a little while, however, I was only half-listening to her because I was engrossed in watching television. My mom could see I was preoccupied, so she said, "Okay Rinpoche, you watch TV, and I'll go out." That really distressed me! I thought my mom was leaving me home alone to walk by herself. At first, I felt anger. Then I noticed that I felt sadness at the thought of being angry with my mom, who only wished to share some time with me. I hadn't even considered her. I then felt gratitude for being able to see how my self-centered thinking had caused me to feel irritated. My epiphany caused me to race out the door so I could walk with my mom. She was so happy, it made me happy. It's a precious moment when you can clearly see your own ignorance and change your course of action. At the first sign of afflictive emotions such as anger or greed, try to see if you are standing in your own way of happiness. Have you forgotten to consider others, or are you lost in self-centered thinking?

Being self-focused can be the result of old impressionable memories, or imprints. The reason people see things so differently is because of their different memories. The impressions that past events leave in a person's mind causes different people to view the same object differently. Take, for example, birds. One person may see birds as a great symbol of freedom. Another person may take a more neutral stance and see birds as those things that fly in the sky. Yet another person might have watched Alfred Hitchcock's horrifying movie *The Birds* and now quake at the sight of one. It all depends on your memory. I, for one, have a terrible memory of birds, which is why I am terrified of them, but we'll go into that later. The point is that we perceive things differently based on these impressionable memories; they have conditioned us into thinking about something—even ourselves—in a certain way. This is one of the reasons you have challenges in perceiving things clearly; it contributes to your ignorance about how you actually exist in the world. And you think everyone thinks like you do, which is why differing points of view are so important. Other people's points of view help broaden the way you perceive things and problem solve. Clinging to your point of view is likely to exacerbate your ignorance, take you further from the truth, and give you a bad case of GAS.

This reminds me of an old tale about some blind men and an elephant. There were once six blind men who went to see an elephant. Each of the blind men touched a different part of the elephant: one touched the trunk, one the ear, one the tail, one the leg, one the side, and one the ivory tusk. Then they argued about what the elephant looked like; each thought they knew the whole picture from the part that they had come in contact with. "I felt a fan," claimed the man who touched the ear. "You're wrong; I discerned that it's a broom," asserted the fellow who touched the tail. "That's not right; I sensed it was a snake," professed the guy who felt the trunk. "None of you have it right. I made out that it's a spear," professed the gentleman who encountered the tusk. "No, I detected a wall," stated the one who touched the elephant's side. "That's wrong too; I discovered that an elephant is a tree trunk," affirmed the man who handled the leg. A fan! A broom! A snake! A spear! A wall! A tree trunk! Since they all had differing points of view, they argued among themselves for some time. All the loud arguing woke up a prince napping nearby. In an effort to get them to quiet down, he loudly stated that they were all wrong. "You must put all the parts together to know what an elephant really is!" he shouted. Truth is like that. Your point of view is an important piece of the puzzle, but it isn't the whole puzzle. For the full truth, you mustn't think in terms of your own narrow point of view. Instead, consider the many pieces that make up the one picture.

Let's reflect yet again on the 2020 toilet paper shortage. I am sure you depended on the store having toilet paper, yet when you consider this deeply, you were counting on more than just the store. You were relying on the employees to stock the toilet paper. The store owner to purchase the toilet paper. The trucker to transport the toilet paper. The manufacturer to make the toilet paper and the trees that the toilet paper came from. There are many contributing factors and people involved in getting goods and services. If one link in that chain is broken, then you're back to staring at those empty shelves, asking, "Why me?" Really, what you need to start asking is, "Why us?" Because you are not in this world alone—and most of us get GAS now and then.

## Reflection

A large, hungry canine trotted by the riverside with a piece of meat dangling from his mouth. As he was making his way down the river's edge, he caught sight of his reflection on the water's glassy surface. In his ignorance, he assumed that his reflection was another dog with meat. Thinking how nice it would be to have twice as much to snack on, the mutt got greedy and decided to steal the other dog's food. Ready for a fight, he growled angrily and bared his teeth. When he opened his mouth to snatch the extra grub, the meat fell into the river and sank to its murky depths. The dog irritably paced back and forth, then hungrily slunk away in defeat.

There's a strong link between self-cherishing and your GAS. Reflect on a recent experience that made you feel miserable. You'll likely find that it resulted from greed, anger, and stupidity rooted in self-attachment. To reduce your GAS, you must find ways to break the habit of always thinking of yourself first. You do this by cultivating the habit of thinking about the needs of others, especially those closest to you. How do you become more concerned for others? First, it would be best if you got out of your way. As a practice, you must hone in on your ability to recognize self-attachment as soon as you experience it and then make an effort to think of others. Try it out at the dinner table.

When the cook has set out all the food, take a pause. Deliberate, then consider your habit of self-cherishing. Don't immediately become concerned only with what you want. Resist the urge to take the best-looking piece of fruit, be the first to be served, or eat the most. And from time to time, when you find it difficult to see past yourself, you can even reflect from the perspective of your own self-interest. You can think about how the more you're interested in the welfare of others, the happier *you'll* be. When you are around others and concerned about their needs, they'll respond in kind, making you happy. It's just that simple.

At the first sign of GASSY self-cherishing, try the following antidotes:

**Greed.** Perhaps, like the greedy dog who sees its reflection, you are not happy with what you have and want what others have. When you desire things, remember that material possessions are not the source of genuine happiness; your healthy state of mind is the source. Generate a healthy mental disposition by reflecting on what you do have, rather than what you "lack." Consider your blessings. You have the good fortune of having things that others don't, things like comfortable shoes and clean water. Feel appreciation. Then, as you are able, practice developing a spirit of generosity. You needn't give material possessions, especially if you have meager resources. Offering kindness and gratitude is a great place to start.

**Anger.** Anger, or hatred, is the opposite of loving-kindness. It is a destructive emotion that directly harms you and those around you, so you must challenge it immediately. That is not to say that you won't feel anger. Irritability happens, so you needn't feel guilty if you do get bothered. Anger itself is not destructive; what you do with its energy is what counts. It would help if you learned how to transform the forcefulness of anger into tranquility. Tibetan Buddhism offers a variety of methods to do so. One of these is from the Dzogchen tradition of Tibetan Buddhism, a helpful practice called sky gazing. When you look up at the sky, you connect to a vast, open, expansive space. This boundless expanse is the primordial nature of your mind—its natural state before all the mental conditioning and ego building.

Seeing the vast sky induces tranquility and joy. You can use a practical version of sky gazing to challenge the energy of your anger. First, it is essential to give yourself a moment to practice. If you are in the company of others, especially if they are the target of your anger, let them know you need a moment to think, then find a private space. Second, direct your gaze by lifting your chin slightly and rolling your eyes up as far as possible. Third, envision a broad, expansive sky if one is not available before you. (If you can't get away from others, you can make looking upward seem like you're in deep thought. Perhaps that won't be *too* off-putting to those around you.) Looking up helps distract and open your mind—it takes both your mind and your eyes off whatever it is that is making you angry. Fourth, bring your attention to your breath. Take a deep breath in, and on the out-breath, let go of what is causing you stress. Release it into the vast sky. In old photographs of Tibetan yogis, you notice that they often practice sky gazing. The practice of looking upward, especially into the wide-open heavens, frees your mind of thoughts. We all know that if somebody says something that bothers us, the more we think about it, the more annoyed we become. This method is a way of cutting through such unproductive thinking. If you practice this regularly, things will start looking up.

**Stupidity.** Ignorance is the result of not knowing the truth. It is living in darkness without the light of wisdom. When you're blind like this, it is challenging to see that you need a better understanding of reality. Unfortunately, you're attached to your selfish cravings, which keep you in the dark, asleep. To wake up from your selfish daydream of having things a certain way, regularly remind yourself of your propensity to be unconscious. Practice being aware of what is happening outside of yourself. Focus on this present moment. Use your breath as an anchor. As you become more attentive to the here and now, you witness how self-centered you can be. Be heedful of your self-focused behavior and try to shed some light on your selfishness. Live smarter and become conscious of how harmfully obscuring your self-cherishing can be.

# CHAPTER 3

# Hope, the Remedy for Hard Times

I T WAS thought that the western monarch butterfly was near extinction when in 2021, the population made a significant surge. Things in life ebb and flow; still, the return of the monarch butterfly clearly signals hope! But then again, butterflies have always been a powerful symbol for hope and transformation. The butterfly reminds us that although the stages of life may be hard to endure, and sometimes dark, if you stay the course, something unique emerges, then soars. Be that as it may, there would be no majestic butterfly if it weren't for the lowly, creeping caterpillar. Hope starts with accepting one's own caterpillar stage. A caterpillar's first task and primary job is to undulate around and eat so they can build energy for transformation. If you do that, then you'll give consumerism a whole new meaning. Of course, that's not what I'm asking of you. What I mean is that change begins with accepting the truth; it starts with that beginning, humble stage. If it weren't for your past and the suffering you've experienced, there would be nothing to transform. The fact is that suffering is a part of the reality of life, so to transcend your misery you need to generate a powerful sense of hope. This type of trust I'm suggesting is not just another form of wanting. It's not merely wishful thinking. It's hopeful knowing that fuels your movement toward positive metamorphosis.

## HOPE STARTS WITH THE TRUTH

So how can you develop genuine hope? You must start with the truth. The first step is to accept and recognize that although life is wonderful, it also has hardship and pain. It is essential that you gen-uinely comprehend that life is a mixture of suffering and joy; the two go together like two sides of a coin. Is there such a thing as a one-sided coin? It would be unrealistic to expect a life of all hap-piness and no sorrow because that's impossible! Things exist in relation to other things. For example, the dark exists in relation to the light; literally and metaphorically, the rainbow is there because of the rain. Opposites exist everywhere. Some people assume that I'm always smiling and laughing because I never suffer. They see my happy demeanor and think, "What a joyful fellow. I wish I could be as happy as he is, but unlike his life, my life is far too difficult for me to be that happy." In fact, I, too, face lots of difficulties. However, I run on truth and the hope of transformation; I'm confident of change, which motivates me to find reasonable solutions to the problems in my life. All people have issues and troubles, but you, too, have the power and strength of hope inside of you.

I've witnessed this strong hope in young children. My monastery in Nepal houses many orphans. About forty percent of our students have nowhere to live, and one hundred percent of them are impov-erished. Some of their stories are quite sad. For instance, not too long ago, a tiny, downhearted child was escorted into my office. This courageous little kid walked up to my desk and handed me a piece of paper that he held tightly in his fist. I looked at the child, who had such a somber look on his face, then down at the crumpled piece of paper he handed me. What he handed over was his mother's death certificate. After doing some investigation, I discovered that this little child's father had already passed away, and he didn't have any other family members or friends able to care for him. He was, in the truest sense, an orphan. I took this kid in, and though it took him some time to adjust, the child's fear and sadness slowly began to transform into a feeling of safety and, more importantly, hope. Sometimes even the bravest of us can feel alone—but let me assure you, you are not alone. All of us are in this together.

Hope unifies communities because it helps enable trust. My mon-astery takes in a lot of orphans with similar stories, and it never ceases to amaze me that these children, with few resources, develop a tremendous amount of belief that their lives will get better. We give them a place to stay, food, clothing, and an education, which help support their basic needs. However, it's their hope that has encouraged trust among them and, in turn, generated beneficial, empowering cooperation. The orphans now feel as though they are one big family. These small children had no choice but to accept their caterpillar stages. By working with the truth of their lives, they simultaneously generated hope. For a fact, hope begins by first accepting the truth that everyone encounters hardships that can be unsettling. But once you can see hardship as an ordinary, conquerable setback, your despair will give way to hope's motivating force. You can then generate healthy solutions around your problems. There are quite a few people that feel hopeless. They find their problems too hard to accept, to the point that it becomes a burden for them to go on living. To make matters worse, they assume their particular problem is unique to them and permanent. As a result of having no hope, they feel the only way out is through death. I strongly encourage you to seek medical attention if you've reached this point.

Let's take a moment to ponder the facts of just how life-threatening lacking hope can be. According to the World Health Organization, one person commits suicide every forty seconds. That is fifteen people every ten minutes, or ninety people each hour. Clearly hopelessness is an enormous issue worldwide. This human tragedy is even more prevalent during hard times. I make an effort to know these facts because a big part of my job is counseling troubled, hopeless people. Once, I was asked to assist a young man around twenty-one years of age. This young man was brilliant, attended a university, and had a good life and a bright future. He was doing exceptionally well in school but was troubled, so I hoped to help him feel better. Sadly, before I could be of service to him, he took his own life. This encounter opened my eyes to how widespread suicide is and how intense the grief is for friends and family left in its wake. I sincerely wish I could have helped that bright, young man; his death deeply saddened his friends and family. It saddened me too.

In the previous chapter I described death as a passage to another sort of life. But once you have passed, you have lost the golden opportunity to solve your problems in this life. I believe that we live an endless number of lives—so why not solve these problems now, in this lifetime? You don't want to miss the chance to make your existence better; you have the rare occasion and the ability to do so in this precious human life. Commit to waking up to this invaluable gift, to generating hope. Consider the natural miracles this life offers: the beauty of a flower, the brilliance of a sunset, the sweetness of an apple, and the warmth of love and compassion. That your body breathes on its own accord, even while asleep, is one of life's many miraculous blessings. Let these miracles motivate you; have hope! You have the power to make changes in the right direction. To do so requires a shift in focus from caring mainly for oneself to caring for the world around you. When you shift your focus like that, your mind stops ruminating on yourself and your own problems. And at that point, there is no "you" to hurt, harm, or eliminate. Removing the misconception of an independent self from your mental landscape generates a wide, open space for the truth of your interdependence to enter. Just like the orphans, you benefit significantly from changing your focus from self-pity to other-empowerment, from focusing on your problems to instead considering giving hope to the entire community. Knowledge of your oneness breeds confidence. Confidence breeds hope. I recall a story that illustrates well how this is accomplished.

## THE SEED OF HAPPINESS IS HOPE

There was once a miserable, wealthy man who spent most of his time alone. His wealth did not make him happy. He wondered what the source of happiness was. He heard that he must learn to be good to others to be truly joyful, but he didn't know where to start because his mind was preoccupied with selfish desires. Desperate for a way out of his misery, he decided to hold a contest. He offered one hundred pieces of gold to the person who could help him answer the three critical questions necessary for altruism: Who should he be good toward? When should he do this? What should he do to be good to another person? For a long time, he did not receive a satisfactory answer, which deepened his despair. Seeing his desperation, a townsperson felt compassion and encouraged him to keep seeking for his answers and not give up hope. She suggested that he ask the wise old woman down the road, as certainly a sage could help him on his quest for joy. So he sought her out, hoping that her answers could help lift him from his anguish.

Once he found the wise woman, he asked for her help. She smiled and joyfully said he would have the answers to his questions within a week and then implored him to stay optimistic. After she spoke, some unsuspecting villager was shot and wounded by a stray arrow while walking past the two of them. Seeing the wounded man's pain, the woman insisted that the wealthy man care for, clean, and bandage the man's injury, then nurse him back to health. Certain that by doing so he'd get the answers he sought, he did as she requested. He provided healing and comfort despite his own discomfort. He took great care in nursing the injured man back to health, and over time, the two formed a friendship. Once the man's wounds were healed, he expressed his deep appreciation, told his new friend not to give up his quest, and then left town. The villagers marveled over the rich man's selfless spirit. "Keep up your search for happiness!" they exclaimed.

For reasons the wealthy man could not pinpoint, he felt so much happier, lighter, and content, yet he continued his plea for answers to his three questions. "Wise old woman, you told me that I'd receive answers to my questions after one week. I have been patiently waiting for answers for *two* weeks. I am desperate to find my way out of darkness. I would like to be happy. Would you please tell me the answers?"

She looked at the man kindly but inquisitively and stated, "My dear, the world already answered your questions. To help you understand the answer to your first question, who should you be good toward? The answer is that you should be good to the person right in front of you. To your second question, when should you be good to them? The answer is that you should be good to them right now.

To your third question, what should you do to be good to others? The answer is you should do everything in your power." The man reflected and discovered that selfish desires never make someone happy. Being unselfish and doing all you can to help those you encounter is what brings true happiness. Upon deeper reflection, he discovered that the seed of this joy really lies in hope. If it weren't for his hope for happiness and the hope that the villagers gave him on his way, he might not have sought answers to his suffering at all. Hope ignites your quest and helps you persevere. The man laughed joyfully. Feeling grateful and extremely content with the answers, he gave the woman three times the gold he had promised, and rumor has it he remained hopeful, helpful, and happy for the rest of his days. GAS kept him miserable, as afflictive emotions often do, but his hope empowered him to seek the happiness that being good to others brings. There is a well-known Chinese proverb that states, "If you want happiness for an hour, take a nap. If you want happiness for a day, go fishing. If you want happiness for a month, get married. If you want happiness for a year, inherit a fortune. If you want happiness for a lifetime, help somebody else." Taking a close look at this proverb you can see it first considers all the worldly, selfish pleasures before showing that true, lasting happiness can only be found through helping others. Helping others helps you but helping others starts with hope. Hope for a better world.

## HOPE AND FEAR

Hope begins on the mental level. Before you can even help others, it must be a wish in your mind. It must be an aspiration you have inside of you for a better life for yourself and others. Unfortunately, fear can interfere with hope. Among all the destructive emotions, fear is one of the worst because it can kill hope. Both hope and fear are felt in anticipation of something. Although both are motivators, it is fear that causes one to worry, panic, and back away from an outcome. Hope encourages a person to move toward and aim for a particularly positive result. Some fearsome thoughts are rational, like the alarm you feel when your car's tire gives out while driving. That type of fright keeps you safe, but most anxieties don't help you because they are learned and based on the fight-or-flight response.

My earliest learned apprehension, strange as it may sound, was the possibility of encountering an owl. I always wanted to stay up late when I was an energetic young boy. Since I didn't go to bed when I was supposed to, my mom developed a tactic to get me to go to bed. She said that if I didn't get to sleep, an owl would swoop down and take me away. This image terrified me! I was afraid of being snatched up by a hungry owl, and that terror motivated me to go to the safety of my bed. Because of this and other frightening encounters with birds, I developed an intense apprehension whenever I encountered them. I felt so scared in their company and desperately hoped for my fear to go away. When I got older, I learned ways to take responsibility for my fear. I trained my mind by envisioning myself befriending my feathered enemy. Anytime I encountered a bird, I had to first generate hope on the mental level. I imagined myself petting and caring for it so that it no longer wanted to make a meal of me. The more I practiced, the less fearful of birds I became. But it wasn't long before another apprehension replaced it. As the saying goes, there is nothing to fear but fear itself. That is because the worst part of being frightened, apart from dashing your hopes, is that it becomes a bad habit.

It's like the tale of the man who was terrified of ghosts. He and his family lived next to a gloomy, spooky cemetery that caused his imagination to run wild. Anytime he heard the slightest crack or creak in his home, he was sure that it was a ghost. Desperate to get rid of these noisy spirits, he sought a remedy. He found a shop in his town that specialized in paranormal activity. The salesman suggested that he purchase an expensive but powerful locket that trapped ghosts inside its hollow center. He assured the man that it would keep the annoying apparitions contained as long as no one opened the locket and released them. The man purchased the locket and sped home, eager to finally rid his dwelling of those pesky ghosts.

The locket worked like a charm for a while. But one day he came home and noticed his curious young son was playing with it.

Obviously, the terrified man took the locket away and warned his son that it must never be opened! Weeks passed, and the man ran into the salesman who sold him the locket. The salesman asked him if the locket helped with his fear of ghosts. The guy anxiously replied, "The locket you gave me was effective in ridding me of my fear of ghosts. However, now I fear that my son will accidentally open the locket and release these encapsulated spirits!" Fear can be a bad habit. Once one fear leaves, another can quickly replace it.

Fortunately for you, hope can dispel fear. That is because hope builds courage and strength to face the truth with optimism. Once I was on a flight to New Delhi. There were about fifteen other passengers aboard. Suddenly, we experienced heavy turbulence accompanied by bright flashes of lightning. Lightning flashed so close to the plane that one of the flight attendants started screaming loudly. People were panicking as they faced one of their biggest fears: the fear of death. At first, I was also afraid, thinking that the airplane would be struck down and descend in a fiery blaze of light. But then I shifted my focus and used mind training practice to allay my fears and generate hope. Initially I reminded myself that nothing lasts forever; death is inevitable and natural. I felt hopeful that my years of living right and being of service to others would pay off in the end. A feeling of gratitude washed over me as I considered the ways that I had mentally prepared myself for death. Thinking in this manner calmed me and gave me hope. After ten minutes, we landed safely at the New Delhi airport, but I still felt rattled. This is why it is so important to prepare yourself for death. Life is uncertain, but death is certain, so you must prepare to face that moment with hope, not fear.

I am appreciative for having that death-defying experience. I now know how others feel who go through something similar. When I see an airplane flying high above, I always wish for the passengers to have a safe, smooth flight to their destination. Using your mind training practice, in this case the practice of impermanence, can help you generate the hope for a positive outcome. Hope gives you courage. A big part of courage is accepting the way things really are and then working with that truth in your mind. Courage can get you through some very frightening moments. You must build a solid belief in yourself and your ability to boldly overcome your problems.

## BELIEVE IN YOURSELF

This self-belief is intimately related to hope and happiness. Each is equally important, so you must clearly understand their relationship to one another. To be happy, you must trust yourself. Believing in your ability to care for yourself and problem solve is the foundation upon which hope and subsequent happiness rely. So how do you build strong self-belief? You first must know what self-belief is not. Self-belief is not being self-centered or selfish. It is not arrogance. Self-belief is having faith in your human capabilities.

From a scientific perspective, by virtue of your highly developed human brain, you have the intelligence to understand and overcome fundamental problems. But what is your mind's role in your brain's ability to problem solve? The brain and mind are often used interchangeably yet differ considerably. The brain is an organ related to the nervous system and has a shape; you can examine it and conduct studies based on its capabilities. The brain is like a computer's hardware. The mind, however, doesn't have a material aspect like the brain; it has no discernable shape, weight, and size. Instead, it is more like energy, and in that way is more like the computer's software. Your brain and mind work together to assist in problem-solving. Both contribute to your ability to effectively handle challenges. Brain and mind research is a burgeoning field at places like the Center for Mind and Brain at the University of California, Davis. Scholars are exploring the relationship between the mind and its influence on the brain, and vice versa, in areas such as development and aging, as well as cognitive, social, and emotional processes. Even though science has long explained the processes of the brain and many physical phenomena, scientists are now developing a body of research on the relationship between the brain and your mind. I believe both play a key role in your ability to tackle difficulties and consequently build self-belief. And the more that the scientific and medical communities study this field, the greater our potential to tap into the tremendous power of the mind.

As a Buddhist teacher, familiarizing myself with how a sentient being's mind works is an important part of helping people. I believe in the power of mind. Every form of mental activity comes from your mind. Your mind is always changing as it busily works with your life experience. Buddhist practices focus on this mental aspect of your being. Practices such as quieting your mind, familiarizing yourself with your mind, and transforming your mind are all common and assist with your problem-solving capability. It is the mind's activity that is responsible for the development of positive emotions such as caring, compassion, gratitude, and love. It is also responsible for negative emotions. Buddhists make both an objective and a subjective study of their own mental activity. Because your mind determines how you experience life, my tradition focuses heavily on training one's mental energy. That is why the contemplative exercises at the end of each chapter have great power. The mind's energy is incredibly powerful and plays a primary role in shaping your world.

Do you believe in your mind's power? Do you have faith in your capability to rise above any issue you encounter? It's easy to lose sight of your mind's ability to shape your life for the better. That is why I urge you to engage in mind training practices. In between mind training practices it is important to regularly remind yourself that your life is what you make it. Ask yourself: Will you make lemonade out of lemons? Or will you wait for oranges? Maybe you'll wait for someone else to make lemonade for you. You may have to wait a long time. It's best if you take responsibility for your life and solve your own difficulties. You are your own hero. You are the only one who is in the position to change your life, because both the problem and the solution are within you. Believe in yourself. When you were a tiny baby, you had no choice but to trust your mom or your caregiver. Now that you're grown, you must transfer that same level of trust to yourself. It is imperative to have faith in yourself. Trust yourself no less than one hundred percent! Always remember that solid hope is grounded in the belief that you can handle the truth and any problems that might come with it. Hope grounded in the truth like this is unshakable.

False hope, on the other hand, is *not* grounded in the truth. It typically is generated by lying, especially to oneself. It's a confident feeling about something you wish to be true but isn't. When I was a professor at Sera Jey Monastic University, I conducted classes for lay students at universities, public facilities, temples, and medical facilities. Some people came to my classes because they were curious about Buddhism. Most people who attended were seeking advice on how to live a better life. I recall meeting with a physician while teaching a class at Linkou Chang Gung Memorial Hospital in Taiwan. He wondered if false hope could be helpful to his patients; he asked me if it was wrong to tell people that they were doing better, even though they weren't, in order to get them to continue their medical treatments. I suggested he be honest in order to not give his patients false hope. Although his intentions were to help encourage them, the truth would encourage them another way, by giving them the opportunity to take a different course of action. How can they hope to get better if they don't know the truth of their situation? If the patient knew the truth, they could then seek different, possibly better, healing methods. Or perhaps they could simply start knocking items off their bucket list. It's their choice. False hope can keep you on an ineffectual course of action. Real hope is based on the truth. To make lemonade out of lemons, you must possess the "lemons"— that is, the power of reality.

When you acknowledge what's real, you have a true shot at building the self-belief necessary for genuine hope. I once read a great book about an incredible, well-known police detective who specialized in antiterrorism. This detective was amazingly skilled at his job. For example, he managed to catch all the people involved in a particular bombing within forty-eight hours of the incident! He wrote a book about his life-threatening exploits and achievements. At the end of the book, he wrote something straightforward but so meaningful, essentially saying that if you really have the truth on your side, in the end, you will be victorious. This is incredibly important to know! If he didn't know the facts of a case, how could he possibly succeed in solving it? So many of us get caught up in fabrications and the false hopes they generate. Knowing this, we should value and respect the power of truth. If we did, we would have the strength of certainty. You must start by accepting reality so that you will be able to make smart choices. Making smart choices will build your self-belief. This is something that you must do even if it's initially uncomfortable.

At the monastery, we even make sure to tell the orphans the truth. We take many abandoned children into our monastery. But we also accept children who have the support of family members. Occasionally the children with family members may receive a small gift by mail. They don't receive anything extravagant because all of our students' families are impoverished; they usually receive something like an inexpensive watch. This can make the children without family feel left out. The school staff and teachers are so often torn on what to do. Even so, it is their decision to tell the orphans the truth, that they will not be receiving a little gift in the mail. This is not to hurt their feelings but to encourage them to accept how their lives really are. Once they learn their reality they can then work with it. That is what you must do, too. You must be okay with caterpillar stage and work with that truth. It is not helpful to hide from reality or lie to yourself. If you can accept the facts of your situation, there is hope for a way forward.

Truth enables you to respond well. For example, most people are afraid of the cobras found around the monastery, mainly because they do not understand the nature of cobras and how they behave. The truth is, a cobra will not attack you unless it feels threatened; if you keep a safe distance, it will not bite you. Truth, and the knowledge it brings, is far more helpful to you than pretense.

The truth is that life has problems and suffering. You can't escape that fact. The great news is that the world we live in is flexible and dynamic, so no matter what problems you have in your life, they are subject to change. There is hope because transformation is guaranteed.

Let's remember the butterfly, the powerful symbol of our ability to positively transform. Like the insect's development from caterpillar to chrysalis, the stages of your life may be difficult to endure, too, but nothing lasts forever. If you develop a strong belief in your ability to transform your life, you generate hope, and with that hope you can metamorphose your life for the better. But you mustn't forget that change begins with the truth—the truth that everything is changing.

Helen Keller, who was blind and deaf, honored the butterfly's transformation as a symbol of hope when she wrote, "One can never consent to creep when one feels an impulse to soar." Despite the challenges of her disability, Helen Keller accepted the reality of her situation, the truth of the caterpillar stage. She believed in her ability to overcome problems and thus learned to communicate in a way that best suited her circumstance. Because of her self-belief, she achieved outstanding success as a well-known author and advocate. Her example reminds the world that no matter how great your challenge is, through accepting reality, developing powerful self-belief, and generating hope, you can work with your mind and transform any problem for the better.

Some people believe that time heals all wounds, but it's the change that occurs with the passage of time that truly cures what ails you. Whenever you encounter a problem, reflect on its impermanent nature. Recall that problems are not solid, unchangeable things but can be overcome precisely because they are not permanent.

## Reflection

A thirsty deer with large antlers decided to drink from a pond. The deer glimpsed his reflection on the water's surface. Initially, he admired the majestic rack on his head, but then his attention quickly shifted to his hopelessly scrawny legs. He didn't like his weak, spindly legs at all. Just then, an arrow flew from the nearby bush. In a flash, he bounded into the woods. Realizing that he survived thanks to his skinny legs, he glanced downward to gaze at them. As he did, his antler caught, trapping him to a sturdy tree branch. Another arrow flew out of the brush, killing the poor beast. Unlike the deer, please don't wait until it is too late to develop the belief that you are more capable than you know.

To avoid falling victim to hopelessness, you need to remember that each of us has potential within ourselves. This potential is called "buddha nature." The Buddha explained this as the innate ability all sentient beings possess to overcome all suffering. This potential is in all beings, regardless of their belief system. Feeling confident in your potential is tantamount to recognizing the inherent power inside of you. A good understanding of your true nature encourages self-belief and is a cause for hope.

Some say hope is not helpful because it's just another form of desire, which is something to be relinquished, but true hope is not wishful magical thinking. It is understanding the practical truth that you will encounter problems, and you are capable of solving them. It would help if you continually reminded yourself that your life is what you make of it. There is no need to rely on someone other than yourself to change your life. You are the only one who can improve your existence because, ultimately, both the problem and the solution are a matter of your mind.

In his very first sermon, the Buddha taught the four noble truths. The first truth tells us that suffering exists; the second, that there is a cause for suffering; the third, that suffering is not permanent, it does have an end; the fourth, the way to end that suffering is by generating the cause to bring about its end. You can generate these helpful causes by following the eightfold path. The path emphasizes three primary aspects: wisdom, wholesome behavior, and mental concentration. It encourages right "being" and goes as follows: Know the truth, free your mind from impure thoughts, refuse to say hurtful words, work for the good of others, have a livelihood that is respectful of life, make the effort to live ethically, practice concentration by developing focus, and practice to control your thoughts. In consideration of the entire sermon, you could say that "find the source of suffering" is the first and most effective mantra the Buddha gave us. These four noble truths are the framework to be applied to our own experience. Use the four noble truths as a method to find a solution when you encounter a problem. First, identify the problem by considering the nature of the difficulty. Second, take some time to reflect on what caused the problem. It is essential to identify and be clear about the real root cause of your situation so you can find a suitable solution. Are you just trying to get things your way? Is your GAS problem the cause? Third, remind yourself that you have buddha nature and can solve this problem. Fourth, you can't control others, but you can take full responsibility for your problems by applying the three aspects of the eightfold path: wisdom, wholesome behavior, and concentration. Consider the following:

**Wisdom.** Do you have the knowledge necessary to solve the problem? Is your intention a pure one? Are you speaking honestly about the issue, or are you perpetuating myths?

**Wholesome behavior.** Are you actively doing what's necessary to solve the problem? Are you avoiding a lifestyle that is counterproductive to the solution? Are you applying a strong effort to solve the problem?

**Concentration.** Are you being present so that you can recognize the problem and tackle it when it surfaces? Are you focusing your attention on the solution?

# CHAPTER 4

# Breaking Free from Self-Deception

W HEN YOU open a bag of chips and look inside, you may notice that the bag is not full. This is because the extra air prevents the chips from breaking in transit. But for ravenous individuals, this may be a disappointment, so they see the bag as half empty. Those trying to lose some weight might think, "This doesn't look like so many chips; I'm so happy the bag is half full!" Some might even believe that the snack company is out to get them, charging them full price for half a bag, so they might have a chip on their shoulder. It's a glass half empty, glass half full scenario because how you experience existence is a matter of perspective. Your life is a mirror reflecting the state of your inner world.

## POLISHING THE MIRROR

To see clearly you must first polish your mirror to clear it of what distorts the truth: your obscuring self-deception. You're probably thinking that cleaning your mirror is a job you can literally see yourself doing. I say that in jest, however, the Greek mythological figure Narcissus didn't think his reflection was a joke. He couldn't take his eyes off his handsome form mirrored in the water; for him it was a trap. Nothing could tempt him from his self-absorption, which is the case with quite a few people. Narcissus would have difficulty staying in my monastery because our monastic quarters have not a single looking glass. This is sometimes eye-opening to visitors. I recall a specific time when a new student came to stay at the monastery and was completely shocked that there were no mirrors. It was no surprise when this new student excitedly told me, "I can't believe it! I haven't looked in a mirror in two whole days, I've never gone so long without looking in a mirror! I was unaware of just how much I check my reflection." He was flabbergasted. He was no longer looking at the reflection in the bathroom mirror, he was looking at himself in a different way: inner reflection. Self-improvement starts with breaking self-deception and learning to face the truth. You must honestly witness, then evaluate, how your mental, emotional, and behavioral actions obscure the truth. Once you are able to reflect on yourself in this way and are able to see where you struggle, then I can offer my help.

Part of my job as a spiritual advisor is to offer free help to people who are struggling with all sorts of afflictions. I offer free classes, workshops, and study groups at universities, religious organizations, public centers, medical institutions, and on the internet. I have also made myself available for telephone calls and personal visits in some more severe circumstances. Because I am actively involved in helping people worldwide, I meet people from all walks of life. I encounter people who are curious about Buddhism; I come across individuals who are seeking a way of life that is healthy; I connect with those who are seriously suffering with mental and physical ailments. Most all these people are looking for some professional help. It is fortunate for them that from the age of five I have been trained to help others, particularly those who are suffering. My tradition focuses heavily on developing spiritual leaders who dedicate their lives to providing cost-free, efficacious antidotes and remedies for a wide range of afflictions. But before I can help you improve yourself, it is important for you to accurately see your personal weaknesses.

When I led a self-improvement workshop at the Linkou Chang Hung Memorial Hospital in Taiwan, most of the sixty to seventy participants were ordinary people looking to better themselves. I asked them to find five personal shortcomings that they possessed. It was very challenging for them to do this! A few of the participants produced at least three imperfections, the others less; then, one gentleman said, "I think you should ask my spouse." It's much easier for you to point out areas where other people can improve rather than seeing your own flaws. This is how it usually is. You have difficulty looking at your imperfections, so you tell yourself lies, stay in your self-deception, and thus never can clearly reflect on what areas need improvement. Self-reflection begins with polishing your mirror until its free from the stains of such lies. Unfortunately, many of us don't want to look at the truth of our imperfections; we want to stay in denial. But, as the saying goes, denial is not a river in Egypt.

## START BY BEING HONEST

There is no hope of changing your perspective when you deny the truth. That is why it is crucial to steer clear of lying altogether. To completely give up lying is quite tricky. Even trivial lies—like those standard varieties that you tell people to encourage them or make them feel better—must be abandoned. They may seem harmless, but these lies do not help our efforts to break free of self-deception. When you encounter a situation where there is no way for you to tell the truth, it is better to just stay silent. You could, however, skillfully redirect the conversation. For example, you can look at what qualities the person you are talking to truly has and then say something encouraging to them based on that. There are always some good things you can point out. Even if you can't eliminate lies completely, at least try to reduce their frequency. Be strict about it. The very foundation of all practice is moving closer to the truth. You can't do this if you encourage detachment from reality.

Additionally, lying hurts the liar most of all. Often people tell me to say this or that during my teachings such that I feel under pressure to say things that are untrue. Even though I find these situations very difficult, I stick with the truth. So, try hard not to lie and sink yourself further into self-deception. You are the one who will experience the harmful effects of lying.

You may not even have an explicit intention to lie, but somehow a lie slips out of your mouth automatically. Once I went on an auto-rickshaw, which usually only costs thirty rupees. When we returned to the monastery, the driver asked me for five rupees more than the average. As a knee-jerk reaction, I jumped out of the rickshaw then responded by telling him that I did not have five extra rupees. After I entered the monastery, I realized I had a momentary lapse of honesty. I immediately consulted with one of my younger students. I asked, "I just told a lie by mistake, what should I do?" Even though he was very young, he replied, "If you tell someone a lie, you should immediately apologize and try to make things right." What he said was very helpful, so I did a prompt about-face so I could fix my mistake. But it was too late; the opportunity was lost because the driver had already left. I was filled with regret. It is so easy to tell these small, seemingly harmless lies—that is why lying is something you need to be especially mindful of.

It is always off-putting when I am on the receiving end of a "white" lie. There was this nice lady who I hadn't seen in three years. She told me that I looked younger than ever. I know how I've aged, so clearly it was a doozy of a lie. I questioned her trustworthiness. If I bought into her lie, I'd be deceiving myself. Therefore, you must be cautious. To change your perspective for the better, start by being honest. Stay away from lies that deepen deceptions and distort reality.

## Breaking Habits

It's important to be consciously aware that no one is perfect—and neither are you. We are all flawed, and that's what makes us a variety of interesting people. Some of your unrecognized "flaws" are not problematic. Others can cause you a lot of hardship, particularly the ones caused by your habitual tendencies. Insidious, ingrained habits can form from your past actions and experiences. Your past shapes your perception of the present. Suppose you grew up in a place where there were lots of green plants, so you grew comfortable with the color green. You see someone for the first time, and you don't pay close attention to them; instead, you focus on the green shirt they are wearing. Because of this, you get a good feeling about them. Later, however, someone tells you that they are out on parole for murder.

As a result, your perception of that person quickly changes. We all do this. You have certain conditioned tendencies that can blind you to faults, especially your own. These are caused by many different factors, by various causes and conditions, mainly because your life is intimately entwined with everyone and everything around you.

Recall all the people and factors responsible for getting toilet paper to the store. Not one thing exists independently from other things. Likewise, many factors are responsible for building your self-deception. You must consider interdependence and the causes and conditions involved. I will explain this concept more deeply in chapter six; for now, it's good for you to know that these factors contribute to why you mostly see your good points but not your shortcomings. This kind of bias is deep-seated.

You are not who you think you are—you've formed a lot of subconscious habits over the years that are probably unknown to you. That's why you need the input of those you trust, and you need to pay close attention to your thoughts, feelings, and behavior. If you can't see your flaws, there is no self-improvement. All sorts of problems will undoubtedly arise in your personal and professional lives until you develop self-knowledge. However, please do not confuse knowing yourself with focusing only on yourself. Self-knowledge starts with paying close attention to your relationship with the world around you. The good news is that when you reflect on the feedback that you get from outside of yourself with a good measure of honesty, you can see your faults. Keep an open mind and be truthful with yourself. You can clear your mirror, see the truth, then break your self-deception.

## DEVELOPING WISDOM, FINDING PATIENCE

In a way, I am a self-knowledge success story. As a child, I was a bit short-tempered. But when I transformed into a hormonal teenager, I was very temperamental. I couldn't control my anger. In a cringe-worthy yet enlightening moment, I hit and broke a light switch in a fit of rage. That was a vital clue that I needed to work on my temper. Yet it was my mom who made me realize the scope of my irritability.

Once she came over for tea, and my abrupt, unceremonious manner was enough to make her recoil. I then realized the gravity of my grouchiness and how it affected others. Something had to be done about it. I had to be truthful with myself. I had to clear the mirror.

The Tibetan Buddhist tradition focuses on the development of wisdom, which for me began at the age of five. Developing wisdom is not an easy task; you must make sure that you have a correct understanding. In my monastic training, part of this process of developing wisdom is through debate. Buddhist monastic debate helps you remove any misconceptions, assists with the development of the right view, and then strengthens that view through practice. Debate is one part of the path to spiritual wellness. It's a way to get closer to liberation from suffering. In order to be successful, you are expected to verbalize your understanding and then defend it under pressure of cross-examination. You can imagine how well you would have to study to be able to do this.

From ages five to eighteen I attended the Institute of Buddhist Dialectics and then attended college at Sera Jey Monastic University. I studied hard and consequently performed well. One profoundly moving book that I found essential for winning debates was *The Way of the Bodhisattva* by the great monk, philosopher, and poet Shantideva. Not only did his words help me to prove my points, but the chapter on patience personally helped me with my anger. I recall being struck deeply by the chapter's recurring message that nobody is able to live happily with anger. To me, this confirms that that an angry person is not happy now and will not be happy in the future. This is a simple point to understand philosophically, but it is challenging to enact in your daily life because no one chooses anger. Anger just happens based on many factors, causes, and conditions. It is your job to not just recognize when you are angry, but to manage it and then transform it—first into calmness and ultimately into wisdom and compassion.

After some reflection, I realized that passage in the chapter on patience was meant for me and that Shantideva's wise words were urging me to change my temper. You must pay close attention to the world around you. It will act like a mirror and reflect back personal information about you. It is the outside world that gives you tips on how to improve. Shantideva's passage helped me recognize my problem with anger, and it helpfully encouraged my self-reflection. I reflected on my angry thoughts, feelings, and behavior, and as a result, I aimed to be cognizant of my anger in the future. Fortunately for all of us, anger is an emotion that demands your attention, so it's easily recognized. One way to do this is by being mindful of your body. Anger triggers your fight-or-flight response then floods your body with stress hormones. In response to this stress, your muscles tense, your heart rate increases, and you stop breathing deeply. It is essential to train your body first, then your mind will follow.

When I feel irritability emerging, I redirect my mind to my breath, which stops my reactivity. Then I go about breaking the spell of anger by immediately—forcefully, if necessary—shifting my attention to consciously breathing with my diaphragm. I breathe deeply, counting each inhalation and exhalation as one breath: in through the nose and out through the mouth. I slowly count full breaths up to ten, then repeat the cycle until I begin to feel more physically calm. Moving your breath from your chest to your abdomen helps you control your nervous system, encourages your body to relax and your mind to refocus, and brings about a range of health benefits. Over time, I developed a habit of deep breathing under stressful conditions. I kept redirecting my body and mind in this way until my family noticed an improvement in my ability to remain patient. My dad said I changed from a hothead to a calm and collected person. In one year, I had challenged my reactivity and replaced my habitual tendencies to anger with something that calmed me. I am, to this day, much less reactive and far more composed. You can change for the better, too. You can train you mind by making a habit of redirecting your mind in various ways, but first you must see your issues. I hope to help you clear your mirror. I'd like you to see the truth and recognize areas in which you are struggling mentally, emotionally, and behaviorally so you too can work toward self-improvement.

## KEEP AN OPEN MIND

Just like me, I'm sure you would like to have happiness. But to be happy, you must be honest and see what needs to be changed inside yourself. The world around you reflects back, mirroring personal information that can help in this regard. It can also offer tips on where you're struggling and solutions to your issues. Your ego has a way of obscuring areas you struggle with, so you must make certain to consider other people's feedback about you. It's not easy to see your own issues, you need a good, honest person to tell you about them.

When you receive unpleasant feedback, try to resist the impulse to defend yourself with lies or get angry. Don't dirty up your mirror with denial. Take some time to reflect on whether another person's assessment of you and your behavior is correct or not. If you keep an open mind, you can use this as an opportunity to transform a weakness into a strength. Self-improvement is one of the most important aspects of your life, but to do it properly you need a clear mirror—you need honest feedback. I recall a time when someone commented on how tan I was. I hadn't even noticed, so in the restroom, I investigated by looking into the mirror. To me, I didn't look that tan. Perhaps the difference in our perception was the type of lighting, our eyesight, or how clean the mirror was. Keep in mind whenever you get feedback that there are various factors like these to consider. It is all valuable information that you can investigate for yourself. If someone's opinion doesn't hold up to reasoning, then ignore it; but if it does, use it to your advantage. Strive to transform for the better.

## DON'T GET CAUGHT IN THE COMPARISON TRAP

Happiness is based on your state of mind. To illustrate this point, let me share a story that can help you understand how your inner world affects your outer world. I am an avid reader, so whenever I come across a story with a particular lesson, I make certain to commit it to memory. I believe that people learn from stories, particularly if they are amusing. In this story, there was a joyful, contented person who had died and gone to an afterlife in a place of exceptional peace and pure delight. They took full advantage of the incredible benefits of living in such a wondrous, blissful utopia. One day, they chanced upon something that absolutely shocked them: they saw one of their best friends languishing in the local jail. They asked the warden what their friend had done to end up incarcerated in paradise prison. The warden replied, "We had to lock them up. Your discontented friend was sullying our good reputation by disturbing paradise with their boredom, dissatisfaction, and disinterest in bliss. They kept asking to return to Earth so that they could get on their smartphone and surf the internet." If you don't have inner happiness and contentment, not even paradise is enjoyable.

It is important to remember that a person's joy and peace are not based on anything external. Still, people tend to deceive themselves by thinking that happiness can be found outside themselves. They build an impressive physical facade to be admired but disregard the truth of their flaws. Social media is an excellent example of this form of self-deception. Social media reflects only what you desire it to, which is often a narrow, idealized version of yourself. You could use social media to see your tendency to deceive yourself and others, but most people don't. Instead, people feel compelled to compete with the images that others are also projecting.

Our highly competitive modern world has ushered in tremendous technological and material developments. Although this clearly has some rewards, the disadvantages, apart from environmental, tend to be social. Our earthly advancements have led to a strong sense of competitiveness and jealousy. Everyone seems to want to be the top dog. For example, I recall attending a board meeting of a brilliant CEO that I'm well acquainted with. During the meeting he pointed out that his company was doing well by making a decent profit. Then he went on to spotlight the fact that other companies were doing much better than theirs. He kept saying, "Look at how much this company is making! What are we going to do?" He was jealous of the rival businesses because he felt threatened by their success. He thought he had no choice but to compete.

This level of competition can be extremely exhausting and causes unnecessary pressure. It reminds me of an old parable about an ambitious dog, called Pooch, who dreamed of visiting a sacred, famed city far, far in the mountains. One day, bold Pooch set out on the long, arduous journey, expecting it to take no less than one month. The exhausted pup arrived in the city in just two weeks! The few dogs that witnessed this achievement were absolutely astounded. Word spread quickly of Pooch's astonishing feat, and within moments dogs from far and wide gathered around this fleet-footed mutt to ascertain the secret of Pooch's triumphant achievement.

"However did you do it?" they asked in bewilderment. Still heavily panting and dog-tired, Pooch wearily replied, "I set out thinking it would take about a month, with time to stop for breaks. But when I stopped for my first rest, a large pack of dogs started racing with me. That happened each time I tried to take a break. I got very little rest because each time I had to outpace the other dogs just to get a small break!" The other dogs looked on with pity. Pooch heaved one final breath, then collapsed from exhaustion. Poor Pooch died from nonstop competition. Comparison and striving to win are common ways of thinking, but you must consider its detrimental role in your life.

Comparing ourselves to others is part of our human nature—we evaluate ourselves in relation to those around us, something that likely has to do with our survival in this world. Comparisons assist us in assessing where we fit in. According to social comparison theory, developed by the psychologist Leon Festinger in 1954, all people compare themselves to others. Particularly three tiers of people: one tier that we feel is better than us, one that we feel is equal to us, and one that we feel is lesser than us. Comparing yourself to someone you deem more secondary can make you feel better about yourself. Comparing yourself to someone equal is just a way to see how you're holding up to your peers, which has more of a neutral effect. Comparing yourself to those you feel are superior can fuel your jealousy and envy and wreak havoc on your self-esteem. Although this latter type has its roots in survival, it can also generate strong division in our world. To counter this, you must consider how our shared humanity can also serve as a bonding factor.

We humans have a lot in common. Consider our shared vulnerability. If you can see your own vulnerability, you can begin to relate to and have compassion for those less fortunate. When you can relate to others, you needn't resort to making comparisons with them. If you acknowledge your own imperfection, you get that no one is perfect and that we are all prone to struggles. You can then have compassion even for those you believe are better off. To break the habit of self-deception and clear your mirror, you must see our shared humanity. For example, people who live in my native country of Nepal have to endure more and more extreme heat waves every year—but this is a reality across the globe! When you think you're alone in not getting what you want, remember it's the same for everyone. Don't get caught in the comparison trap; instead, remind yourself that we all have challenges in life, no matter which of these three tiers we are on. Once you acknowledge your solidarity with all people, then, and only then, will your comparisons reflect with any accuracy.

## Cause and Effect

Part of self-knowledge is seeing how we humans operate in relation to one another and our surroundings. You are in a relationship with the world around you, and this relationship is based on causality. This means it's a cause-and-effect relationship. Some people use causality to explain away their misfortunes; they may think they have a horrible life now because they did something negative to cause it in a past life. They blame their problems on a case of bad karma. But ruminating on and blaming yourself for some horrible thing you might have done in your past is ineffective; it just doesn't help matters. We all make mistakes.

When you think about it, everyone encounters some misfortune in their lifetime. Every one of these misfortunes has a rational cause.

Naturally, you would like to solve your problems and to find their root source. However, this strong drive to have our problems work out is often why we latch on to the idea of concrete mystical beings who rule our lives behind the scenes. We drum up supernatural ways of eliminating our issues instead of taking personal accountability for them. Some people believe that crystals will heal them of ailments. Sorry, rock lovers; although they are beautiful and magical looking, science doesn't back the healing power of crystals. The Piezo-electric Effect proves that hitting crystals can create electricity and, therefore, they can be used in things like watches and computers. But otherwise, crystals have little effect on you or your life, at least not in a direct sense. What does impact you is understanding that there are specific causes for your problems and distinct solutions for them, too. This requires you to have actual self-knowledge, so you must realize this aspect of your life.

A thorough understanding of how cause and effect work in your own life equips you with real solutions to your problems. For example, about eight years ago, I had some bad abdominal pain. Knowing that the only way I could identify the actual cause of my ailment was by visiting a specialist, I sought out the help of a medical doctor. The doctor asked questions and thoroughly examined me and identified the exact cause that had led to problems with my stomach lining. The physician said I needed to take a break from teaching for two months, rest, and continue to take medicine for nine months. Simply by acknowledging my problem and accepting that reality, I felt better. I was proactively engaging in a helpful course of action and, as a result, I felt good enough to resume teaching within a week. I sometimes still reflect on that incident, wondering what I must have done to cause this ailment—maybe eating the wrong foods or drinking the wrong drinks. Despite considering the causes, I don't get caught up in blame. Blame sullies your mirror of self-reflection. That is why it's important not to focus on blame. Instead, focus on accepting the reality of the problem and do what you can realistically do now. Identify rational causes, then proactively find real solutions.

Similar to the way doctors investigate symptoms in order to diagnose and then treat a specific ailment, you too have the power to treat your suffering. Every kind of suffering can be remedied. To do that you must first clearly understand that there is no such thing as causeless suffering. When you know that wholesome activities have beneficial effects and unwholesome actions have unbeneficial results, you can choose the best for yourself! This means you have a measure of control over your destiny. This is a very precise point that has the ability to remedy any feelings of helplessness. Your actions have actual results, so it's essential to make them count from this point forward.

Once I had a student who thought they might have an unhealthy relationship with food due to stressors in their life. When they experienced difficult situations, they'd stress eat. According to an American Psychological Association survey, approximately one-fourth of Americans rate their stress level as an eight out of ten. Stress releases hormones that encourage overeating. What is worse is that stress eaters tend to eat sugary, high-fat, comfort foods, which makes them even more prone to overeat. In stressful times, many people see the bag of chips half-empty—then eat a couple bags of them. Stress eating is not exclusive to America. Other countries have similar issues. For example, Australia's obesity epidemic is largely driven by emotional eating. Eighty-three percent of overweight or obese Australians blame their weight gain on comfort eating. Regular emotional binge eating leads to weight gain, mental and physical health issues, depression, and anxiety. Fortunately, the first law of thermodynamics says that energy can be neither created nor destroyed; it can only be changed or transferred from one form to another. This is good news! The potential energy stored in your body can be transformed into kinetic energy, so when you get more active, you'll lose any pounds you gained from eating all those chips! I'm being silly, but in truth, rather than focusing on thermodynamics, you must address your relationship with the cause of your stress for any sort of real and lasting change.

Of course, it is not always the case that stress induces hunger. Some people respond to strong emotions by eating more while others eat less, but the cause for both is how they handle stress. So perhaps it isn't an unhealthy relationship with food that is at the heart of the matter, but an unhealthy relationship with stress. You needn't feel guilty about overeating and its effect on weight gain; instead, look at the cause. Once you do this, you can learn to manage your reaction to stress. Take the time to consider and reflect on the cause. Have faith in your ability to find a solution. But as a word of caution, make certain to bypass harsh judgments, blame, and guilt. These cruel assumptions will only deepen your despair and throw you further into self-deception.

Once you clearly witness the cause, set things in motion toward a solution. This will bring about an outcome of your own making. Just like the ripple effect, causality is a process of action and reaction—not only physically, but also energetically and psychologically. Consider, for instance, an example of psychological causation from my own life: hearing that an owl might take me if I didn't go to bed helped me to hit the hay early. But the effect was that I was left with a fear of owls. My unfavorable opinion of birds was further validated by a feisty parrot.

When I was young, I decided to befriend our family parrot. Perhaps it was frightened by my nervousness, but the parrot flapped its wings wildly and squawked at me. Another time it nipped at me with its sharp beak. Because of factors like these in my early childhood, my mirror was smudged: I stopped seeing birds clearly; I just saw them as those winged things that hurt me. To this day if I see a bird harmlessly resting in my path, even at a distance, I have to envision myself befriending the bird, gently holding and petting it. Working with the fear in my mind, I then get the courage to pass by. Visualizing kindness and compassion is a powerful tool. Yet these encounters can also bring up deep memories that have the potential to blanket the truth and further deepen our self-deception. That is the tricky thing about trying to see the truth. The truth is the bird is just a bird, and like the cobra, if you know the bird's true nature, you can intelligently and safely interact with it.

## SEEING THE TRUTH

When we can witness the authentic truth, our direction in life becomes clearer. But getting to the truth is tricky. To illustrate this, take this story of a dedicated hiker who once decided to trek to a beautiful and picturesque plateau in the mountains with his enormous dog. His GPS stopped working halfway there, so he decided to ask someone in a nearby village for directions. Knowing that hiking can be dangerous if you get on the wrong path, the hiker was leery of any misinformation. Accordingly, he sought out guides that could give him the most honest directions and wanted to avoid anyone misleading. When he arrived at the village, he went to the information center and asked if he could meet with a couple of guides. He asked for one guide that was considered honest and one guide who was prone to lying. Before long, the two guides stood before him, wondering what he wanted. He asked them, "I'd like to hike to the plateau and was hoping to get directions from you."

The more honest guide told the man that one would typically have to cross the river to go to the plateau, but since he had his large dog with him, he suggested hiking over the mountain first to get to the plateau. The man prone to lying told him the exact same thing! Since the two guides had given him the exact same answer, he felt that there was no way for him to tell which was the truth. The hiker was baffled, so he headed back to the information center and asked, "If the honest guide and the guide prone to lying said the same thing, how do I know what is true? Are they both lying or telling the truth?"

The center's attendant said, "When the honest guide told you to cross the mountain, this was the truth. When the guide, prone to lying, told you to cross the mountain, clearly, they were telling you a lie." The hiker looked bewildered, so the attendant explained the reasoning. "The guide prone to lying told you to cross the mountain knowing that the easiest way to the plateau is to take the boat across the river. They lied to you because crossing the mountain is not, in fact, the easiest path to take, so their intention was not considerate. The honest guide, telling you to cross the mountain, took your big dog into consideration. They knew you'd have difficulty finding a boat to take you and your dog across the river. Therefore, they encouraged you to cross the mountain in good faith. Really, honesty is a matter of motive. So, in terms of motivation, one guide clearly lied while the other clearly told the truth."

Which is more honest: truth in words or truth in motive? When you want to give up self-deception in favor of self-knowledge, consider the reason why you're doing what you're doing. Reflect on the various factors and hidden motives behind your actions. For, example, some people become doctors in order to make a lot of money, then wonder why they are so miserable, despite all their wealth. Others become physicians because they have compassion for those who are physically ill and want to help them. They love their job, so they feel content. The greater your understanding of this relationship between the truth and accepting the reasons behind things, the closer you are to reality, and thus, the less you'll experience self-deception.

Remember that life is like a mirror: everything you perceive reflects your inner world. Cleaning your dirty mirror of distorting smudges means clearing self-deception and coming closer to the truth. When you get closer to reality, you see that there are reasons why things are the way they are. What you are experiencing has a cause and a resulting effect. Knowing this, examine what causes your happiness. Since happiness is a matter of perspective, ask yourself: Is the bag of chips half empty, or is it half full? Maybe you don't like chips. Regardless, dare to acknowledge the truth and boldly confess your shortcomings without judgment. Only then can you take full responsibility for your life and change what needs changing.

# Reflection

A kind, large water buffalo lived at the edge of the woods. When the sun was high, she'd lay in the shady forest. A mischievous monkey saw the giant beast asleep and decided it would be fun to pull pranks on her. He swung down and pulled the buffalo's tail. She shot up and looked around. "Who was that?" she asked. The monkey muttered, "What a blockhead." All the other monkeys snickered quietly. The water buffalo sought out another shady spot nearby. Once she fell asleep, she felt something hit her head. Once again, she shot up and looked around. Seeing nuts around her, she peered upward and saw the monkey quietly laughing. "Looks like I am not getting much rest today," she said. The monkey pulled several more pranks until the sweet bovid felt resigned to her fate. Seeing the whole thing, a tiny snail said to her, "You're bigger than that monkey; why don't you sock him in the nose?" The water buffalo replied, "Thanks for your concern, little fellow, but I don't want to hurt anybody." The buffalo left the shade of the trees and rested in the sunny field. An ill-tempered buffalo soon took her place under the shady tree. Mistakenly thinking it was the same creature, the foolhardy monkey again pulled the buffalo's tail. This time the buffalo forcefully threw the mischievous primate up against the trunk of a tree. "Ouch!" the monkey cried out. Just as the angry beast was getting ready to trample the injured monkey, the kind water buffalo heard the disturbance and darted in front of him, saving his life. Shocked at her kindness, the monkey responded by saying, "Thanks, but why save me? I really bothered you." The water buffalo replied, "You really are a mischievous monkey, but I'm not like you. I like to treat others the way I'd want to be treated." The monkey saw his fault and was kinder from that day forward.

It is time to clean your mirror. Being able to see your faults plainly and without judgment allows you to see areas where you can improve and make necessary changes. Start by trying to identify five places where you need improvement—and know that this will take time and effort. So many of us are blind to our faults and suffer from self-deception as a result. We see only our good qualities but cannot see what is wrong. At the same time, we're pretty good at noticing the shortcomings of others. This kind of perceptual bias is a deeply ingrained habit. It is also why others are better at seeing what is wrong with us. It takes feedback, introspection, self-honesty, and open-mindedness to identify and then accept our problem areas.

Once you identify the areas where you need to grow, seek out antidotes for each issue. As soon as you find a remedy for a particular problem, immediately put it into practice. If you cannot see where you need improving, ask a trustworthy friend, a family member, or anyone you believe will give you sincere feedback. Ask them to be your *mirror*. Identifying and applying antidotes to at least three problem areas will result in a healthy change in yourself and in your relationships with those you are around. I can guarantee your life will begin to improve. When you hear how others perceive your problematic areas, honestly consider the feedback. Do not automatically reject their opinion or feign ignorance. Be open enough to truly hear the criticism of others. Then impose a boundary around your time on this issue; spend twenty minutes in self-reflection and consider if their feedback is correct. If their words stand up to reason, accept your flaws and work toward positive transformation.

Suppose everyone in your household was open to identifying three or more of their own shortcomings. In that case, can you imagine how everyone at home could undergo a similar transformation, and how happy this would make your home? If you take up this practice with others, be careful not to pressure anyone to change, as tempting as that may be. The only way to convince others of the benefits of this kind of self-improvement is to demonstrate yourself how self-knowledge is empowering. Resolve your issues first; clear the mirror, see the truth, and change for the better.

# CHAPTER 5

# Self-Belief, Not Self-Absorption

THE SCOPE of the universe is mind-boggling! There are more stars in this totality than grains of sand on a beach. Though you might like to think that you're the center of the universe, this amazing cosmos is constantly expanding and has no center. To imply that you think that you're the center of the universe may seem like a harsh accusation, but really it is meant to offer you an empowering insight. For if the world were to revolve around you, the world must be separate. Do you feel separate from this world? I want to assure you that you're not. You're part of a boundless network of interactions; a piece of a vast puzzle made up of causal experiences so interrelated that it is beyond our comprehension. Your physical being exists thanks to the resources on a planet that is about 4.5 billion years old and revolving around a star we call the sun. Many people separate themselves from this world, and consequently, they focus mostly on themselves. They find it difficult to realize their interdependence with a heavenly body that revolves around the sun—and not around them. They may think, "Wow, *I* can't believe that someone would think that *I* think that *I* am the center of the universe. But enough about them!" However, when you really think about the vastness of the universe, you are a relatively small piece of the puzzle. The earth is so tiny, it can fit into the sun 1.3 million times, so imagine how small you are by comparison. How much of this have you absorbed? I hope a lot, but for many of us, it's difficult to genuinely grasp the truth of our place in this universe. As displeasing as this may sound, many of us are just too full of ourselves.

I am not a stranger to self-absorbed behavior. I saw it in my academic career. It was my great fortune to attend one of the best monastic institutes in the world, Sera Jey Monastic University, where I received the equivalent to a PhD in Buddhist philosophy and then became a professor. Since Sera Jey has two different divisions, one for school-age students and another for college students, there were a lot of student monks. Because it was brimming with scholars, I was expected to share my quarters, sometimes with young grade-school monks. During my teaching years, from 1997 to 2015, I noticed two distinct types of students: the clever, crafty kids and the guileless, meek ones. People tended to trust the less crafty students more than the clever ones. I shared my quarters with one young student named Lobsang, who was a very resourceful kid! He was exceptionally keen and observant as well as very cunning. During the holidays, the students get to watch movies. Sometimes they borrow movies from neighboring houses. One time, the students sent out one of the more innocent kids to retrieve some movies on DVD. After searching for quite a while, he came back empty-handed. Then they sent out Lobsang, who was very cunning. He came back proudly toting two piles of DVDs!

I wondered how he got so many movies so quickly. I later found out that he was going around telling everyone that I was the one who wanted the films, and that I wanted them immediately. That is how dodgy this bright kid could be. But it is also the reason why people did not trust him. He lied and was motivated by his own self-interest. They trusted the simpler students more. The artless, humble student seems to naturally have fewer thoughts about himself and knows the world doesn't revolve around him. It's important to use your intelligence— but not for an ego boost or to get your own way. Don't succumb to selfish calculation if you want others to put their trust in you.

## HONEST, NOT PERFECT

As I've noted before, one easy way to catch your own self-centered nature is by looking at a group photo with you in it. If you immediately look at yourself, chances are you're self-absorbed. This happens with virtual video conferencing, too. Do you mainly look at your own image, and make sure the background is just so? I sometimes teach through video conferencing, and on occasion, a playful cat or dog or a curious child joins the lesson. It is healthy to have this authenticity. We are at our best when we are honest, not perfect. But some people don't know this. I recall meeting a woman who was very concerned about her son. Her son and his good friend had recently graduated from college. Not long after, her son's friend started boasting on social media—he posted pictures of his excellent new job, fancy car, lovely house, and other things that showed how his lifestyle had improved. The world revolved around him. Seeing this devastated her son. He had yet to find a job that would benefit him materially, so he became extremely depressed and anxious. He didn't realize that the online world can't show if someone is sincerely happy. Gloating is not an accurate reflection of one's happiness. If you have to brag, chances are you lack self-belief and aren't genuinely happy.

Anyone can post anything online and claim that it is real. Many of us prefer to distort our reality to feel a small measure of self-importance rather than post the truth, which feels less impressive. In doing so, it's easy to lose sight of reality and buy into our own public relations campaign. Furthermore, since so many people around us care about their public image, we are likely to do the same in the spirit of competition. People compare their fake online personas with others' fake online personas. Even video conferencing has a filter option to make you look better. None of us can live up to this type of edited perfection. Comparing your real life with someone's filtered life will only cause insecurity, jealousy, and, resultantly, heavy competition. As for my student's son, instead of being happy about his friend's success, he became self-conscious of what he lacked. He began pitying himself. But when we think of someone who has a big ego, we don't even consider that their self-centered behavior might actually be a result of their feeling of lacking something. You simply can't rely on material possessions as a means to happiness. Instead of comparing himself to his friend, what would have happened if my student's son had felt joy for his friend's success? Then would he have been so anxious and depressed?

## PART OF A COLLECTIVE

Clearly, thinking so much about what you want and what you have—or don't have—only feeds into your neurosis. The more you focus on yourself, the more you suffer. Instead, strive to see that you are on this planet as part of a collective, and each person has an important role to play. Or, as poet John Donne declared, no man is an island. We are all also part of a continent. We are part of one another such that we need one another. How else will you get your toilet paper? Or anything else for that matter, including happiness. It is impossible to be happy if you're only focused on yourself. For sure, you must wring out your self-absorption. I have a perfect story about an insightful person who did just that.

There's an ancient story from the book *Liberation in the Palm of Your Hand* about a famous Tibetan master named Geshe Baen Gung-gyael and the moment when he recognized his self-absorption. Baen had attended an annual gathering where the host was serving large bowls of curd. Curd is a popular dairy product that originated in India, like creamy yogurt. After seeing the scrumptious curd piled on people's plates, Baen eagerly joined the food line in anticipation of eating some. While waiting for his turn, he peered ahead and could see that the host was dishing out enormous spoonfuls to the people at the front of the line. In a moment of selfish dismay, he thought, "Oh no! If they give so much to the people in front, will there be any left for me?" At that moment, he had a profound realization. It dawned on him that he was thinking too much about himself. His self-centered thoughts had developed into greed and made him suffer. After finally making it to the front of the line, the host offered him a large spoonful. Recognizing his selfishness, Baen looked at the host and then turned his bowl upside down. The host asked, "Baen, would you please turn your bowl upright so I can give you some curd?" Baen replied, "No thanks, my selfish mind already ate the curd." Baen witnessed his selfish greed and took a stand against it.

To wring out self-absorption, you must do what Baen did. See it as it is happening and, as the saying goes, nip it in the bud! Shut down the thought, then immediately replace it with an opposing view before it has a chance to grow, get stronger, and become a habit. It's vital that you address your selfishness and then defy it. Occasionally, when I was a college professor, some of the young monks I roomed with used to remind me of this. During apple season, I'd share apple slices with my roommates. Whenever I would take the biggest piece of the apple, they immediately said to me, "Teacher, you took the biggest slice!" Young monks cease to amaze me. They are very keen to point out when someone breaks a rule. When they reminded me that I was behaving selfishly, I was first astounded that these young monks noticed, then shocked that I didn't even catch my own selfishness, then appreciative that they helped open my mind to my unconscious self-absorption. I didn't get defensive. I just felt grateful that the students reminded me to overcome my self-focused habits.

When you get caught in an act of selfishness, try to appreciate that someone points it out to you. Some of us are so self-absorbed that we get defensive when someone contradicts us or our behavior. But defensive behavior only builds a wall between you and the other person. Instead, it's best to be open to others' earnest reflections of our qualities. Consider the way my young students share their honest feedback with me. The remarkable thing about their honesty is when I take the smallest slice of apple, my students say, "Teacher, don't take such a small piece. Please take a bigger piece to eat!" Of course, I listen to them. It's essential to listen to feedback from others!

## ACTIVE LISTENING

Which do you do more of in your daily life, talking or listening? Consider whether you really listen to others or if you focus on listening to your own opinions. When you do listen, do you deceive yourself by selectively hearing only what you want to hear? There was once an employee who kept making a ton of mistakes on the job. It happened week after week. His boss, feeling fed up with his poor work performance, gave him a warning: "If you don't get your act together, I'll have to hire someone else!" Thinking he was a flawless worker, the man responded by saying, "Oh, yes! Do hire someone else! With so much work to do, we sure could use some extra hands around here." The employee was fired on the spot. It took losing his job to see the error of his ways. To live happily in your relations with others, drop your opinions, then listen until you understand. Do not just passively hear their words without considering the significance of them.

To actively listen, you mustn't be so protective of your point of view. Instead, do the contrary: drop your opinions and make an attempt to understand where the other person is coming from. Ask questions for clarification if you must. Family, friends, couples, and communities would all benefit from genuine listening. Take my parents, for instance. Like many couples, my parents occasionally differ in opinion. If my dad feels offended, he shuts down and refuses to listen to my mom. After one such quarrel, I suggested to my dad that he simply listen to Mom instead of shutting down. I proposed that he hear her out instead of disregarding her perspective. He listened to me. At first, this was difficult for him, but it became easier and easier over time. He regularly challenged the supremacy of his opinions and then defied them by opening his mind to another point of view. He now can see that if he gives my mom a chance to speak, actively listens, and understands her, their quarrels quickly resolve. It is not enough to simply hear this advice—you must make a solid effort to catch yourself taking the big slice of apple. Then do the opposite.

This reminds me of the story of a thief and a businessman. There was a sage and caring teacher who would regularly give free, open-air teachings. A businessperson and a thief were both walking by and overheard this phenomenal teacher speaking. Each decided to stay in attendance until the great teacher had wrapped up his lesson. The teacher concluded his lecture with instructions for his listeners to follow. He said, "Keep on doing what you are doing. Continue exactly what you're doing with your life." Upon hearing this, the thief made his way to the teacher to ask a question. He asked, "You said to continue what you are doing with your life, but I am a thief! So, are you okay with what I do? Should I continue stealing for the rest of my life?" The teacher looked at him and repeated, "Continue exactly what you are doing." The businessperson overheard their conversation and thought, "This incredible teacher said we should continue, so I should continue with my business." Another attendee who had been there for the entire lesson heard these words, "Continue exactly what you're doing with your life," and thought the teacher meant just that. Continue attending and listening to the teacher's wise lectures, then apply them to your life.

This shows us how listening is subjective. Some people only hear what they would like to hear, and don't truly listen. When you listen, it is crucial to understand the meaning of what you're listening to. Both the businessperson and the thief were preoccupied with thinking of how they were going to get money. So naturally, they thought the teacher meant they should continue their means of amassing wealth. To understand, you must be present. And to be present, you must stop thinking only of yourself.

## SELF-BELIEF, NOT SELF-ABSORPTION

When you can successfully wring out your self-absorption, you'll be amazed at how much peace and happiness you'll feel. Upon close examination, you'll see that the root cause of your negative emotions, of your GAS, is almost always your self-absorption. That is why it is essential to change your relationship with yourself. That way, you can understand the problem with self-absorption and choose self-belief instead. I've worked with people who have confused self-belief with self-confidence. They may sound similar, but there is a big difference between the two. Self-belief is seeing that you are valuable, that you have inner strength, and that you have a place in this world, just as you are. It is the conviction that you are born valuable. On the other hand, self-confidence lends itself to having a distorted, grandiose view of yourself. Confidence can be based on false notions, so I find the term "self-confidence" problematic.

The "beauty" industry has often made outrageous claims to make people more "self-confident." One time I went to a department store that was selling cosmetics that were supposed to make you look younger. The salesperson encouraged me to try on some type of technology meant for wrinkle detection. She stuck a gadget on my head, which projected my face onto her computer screen. It emphasized the severity of my wrinkles—I could see all of them amplified on the computer image of my face. After pointing out my wrinkles, the salesperson attempted to sell me various wrinkle-reducing products, insisting that that was what I needed to rid myself of these unattractive creases. I then asked her if she wouldn't mind if I saw how her projection looked on the computer screen. As soon as she put the wrinkle detection device on her head and projected her face on the screen, the results were identical. It appeared we both needed some wrinkle-reducing products—even though she was the one selling them and their amazing results!

Frankly, aging naturally causes wrinkles, and no amount of wrinkle cream in the world will make anyone happy. Happiness comes from the inside, yet consumerism tends to be all about the outside. Cosmetics and things of that nature may give you some temporary self-confidence, but they cannot give you self-belief. Through self-belief you possess something undeniable and ingrained. It is a powerful, pure faith in your innate ability to meet life's challenges. It is trusting yourself as you trusted your mother or caregiver when you were a small child. Self-belief doesn't have anything to do with self-indulgence or self-absorption—that sort of self-centered thinking does not lead to happiness. Instead, it has a lot to do with your ability to relate functionally with the world around you. It motivates you to engage healthily with others and to trust your process. It inspires a spirit of kindness and generosity. This unselfishness leads to happiness. Have you ever given something to someone, and it made you feel joyful?

## WHEN GENEROSITY BECOMES NATURAL

When you are not self-absorbed, healthy generosity is natural. A while back, I went to see His Holiness the Dalai Lama. The hosts offered a massive luncheon for all of his visitors. Because there were so many people, lunch was being served at full speed. The line of people hurried along, crowding together to be served. I was no exception. When I finally managed to get served, however, there were so many people that there weren't enough chairs to go around. Eventually, I did manage to find one. But as soon as I sat down to enjoy my lunch, it occurred to me that we were all there so His Holiness could motivate us to work for the benefit of others, not ourselves! I immediately stood up and attempted to give my chair to someone who needed it. The funny thing is, we were all working for the benefit of others, so everyone said to me, "No, please, you sit!" We were all happy to give that chair to someone else.

Generosity inspires hope, builds healthy self-esteem, and has multiple unseen benefits. A sizable amount of scientific evidence now proves that giving promotes well-being, and hence, joy. Giving makes you feel happy. A 2017 study published in *Nature Communications* used MRI technology on participants who pledged to be generous to either themselves or others in order to investigate the link between generosity and joy. They discovered the portion of the brain that is associated with altruism and joy was stimulated when participants practiced generosity by giving to others rather than to themselves. Another study by the National Institute of Health confirmed that when a person gives to charitable organizations, their brain releases endorphins, which then results in a feeling called a "helper's high." Altruistic behavior activates a portion of your brain associated with social connection, pleasure, and trust.

Acts of charity encourage cooperation and social connection. I've seen that when people are charitable and give to others, other people tend to give to them in return. Generosity promotes community trust and closeness, because you see others in a positive light. Giving evokes gratitude, which causes you to feel better about your life and be more optimistic. Generosity is contagious. When people see others being openhanded, it triggers a ripple effect in the community, sowing seeds of hope and kindness as well as encouraging similar behavior among community members. Giving is an excellent example of happiness that comes from the inside. Being openhanded and open-hearted needn't be limited only to gift-giving. You can also be generous with your time, attention, assistance, energy, sympathy, and thoughtfulness. However, I would limit how generous you are with your opinion; giving your two cents is not the kind of generosity I have in mind!

## PUT YOURSELF IN THEIR SHOES

Selfless behavior has a myriad of incredible benefits and is a means of generating joy, whereas self-absorption has the opposite effect. That is why I encourage you to embrace unselfish and good-spirited behavior. Self-absorption is a bad habit. To break this habit of always thinking of yourself, you must think of the needs of others. To do this, start to think from the other person's point of view. Try to put yourself in their shoes. Understanding others' perspectives is a quality that should be nurtured. You encounter everything in your life from your own viewpoint. You may wish to begin to experiment seeing other perspectives in situations that might be considered arbitrary, such as when you determine whether something is delicious or disgusting, or beautiful or ugly. Two people can see the same color but have vastly different judgments of it. If we don't consider outside points of view, subjective, judgmental thinking can interfere with genuine understanding, especially in situations that involve you. This can result in conflict, a lack of appreciation, and a lack of compassion. That's why prior to forming a solid judgment of something, it is necessary to take some time to look beyond your own perspective; suspend your ego, and apply some empathetic understanding.

For example, once while traveling in southern India, I wore a pair of shoes that were far too tight for my feet. I kept thinking about how uncomfortable my feet felt and how I'd like to have a more comfortable pair. Then I saw a poor man who wasn't wearing shoes. I thought of how incredibly uncomfortable it must be for him to walk barefoot on the hot, rocky ground. When I considered that man's perspective, I felt fortunate to have my uncomfortable pair of shoes. As a result, my attitude toward my tight shoes changed. I began to feel lucky to have shoes at all. Sometimes, you may catch a glimpse of another person's perspective, but I encourage you to go further. Place yourself in the other person's shoes—or lack thereof. I urge you to challenge yourself in this way. Take that extra step to broaden your perspective and sincerely sympathize with those around you.

In a world crying out for help, developing sympathy is crucial. To do this, you must break the "me, me, me" habit. But remember that you need some sympathy too. Even if you do think the world revolves around you, it's essential to not be too hard on yourself. Being self-absorbed is usually a result of a felt sense that, in some way, you are not enough just as you are. Perhaps you feel unsafe, alone, or insecure. This could stem from a genetic predisposition, a learned behavior, or perhaps even childhood trauma. Ideally, your positive sense of self-worth starts from birth, from your caregiver's love and attention, and then blossoms with nurturing from your community, family, and friends. But since life naturally has difficulties, many of us do not get this ideal situation. You encounter some hard knocks. When you feel damaged emotionally and psychologically, it can lead to a deficit of self-belief and, as a result, a lot of negative rumination—so much so that it is tough to get out of your own way. But your personal pain can instead be an opportunity for healthy spiritual growth. One surefire way to break the habit of negative self-fixation is to replace it with considering the perspective of other people. Consider the many benefits of your relationship with the world, such as breathing fresh air or drinking clean water. Take this wholesome sentiment a step further and behave in ways that show understanding, appreciation, and compassion toward those closest to you. Generate a habit of wholesome thoughts and deeds. Even if you must at first go through the motions, developing this way of being results in a beneficial transformation within you and without.

* * *

You are a part of everything and have the same aspiration as other conscious beings. You want to be happy. When you understand this about yourself, you can then understand others. Everyone wants joy, yet we all go about getting it differently. This fierce drive to find happiness can result in an unhealthy fixation on your selfish desires. What you must do is catch yourself in the moment when you are lost in self-absorption. To detect your selfish tendencies, make a conscious effort to be aware of your thinking and behavior. You'll want to remain cognizant of your unhealthy habit of repeated self-referral. When you're thinking or talking, are you hearing the word "I," "me," or "my" too much? How much interest are you showing in other people's perspective? Are you monopolizing the conversation? In what ways are you putting yourself in another's shoes? When you're preoccupied with yourself, it is difficult to offer genuine empathy to another person. Try to truly listen to understand them. Once you perceive your selfishness, consider the many wonderful benefits of your relationship with the world around you. In social situations, engage in active listening and make it a point to be present to another's experience. Consciously act in the spirit of surrendering yourself to the moment. If you do this, you will no longer consider yourself the sun. Still, you will undoubtedly be a bright, shiny star!

# Reflection

A mean, miserly man lived in an opulent mansion with a guard dog he didn't bother to name and servants he never got to know. He spent most of his day in isolation, greedily counting his gold. He never invited any other villagers to his stately home. If someone came knocking, he'd irritably turn them away—all the more if they were beggars. The only time he left his house was to collect taxes. On one such occasion, he took his lavish, elegant carriage and guard dog on his collection route. While on his rounds, several brawny robbers confronted him and took all he'd collected and his carriage. They exchanged their ragged clothes for the miser's luxurious ones. Left with nothing, the miser yelled at his canine protector in a rage. "Some guard you are!" he shouted.

After many hours of hungrily wandering in the cold, damp forest, he chanced upon a tiny cottage dimmed by the growing darkness of dusk. Hoping that the inhabitants were charitable, he summoned the courage to knock on the door and ask for a morsel of food and a warm place to sleep for the night. "Come in, dear sir," the friendly man said, welcoming him into his humble one-room house. "Sit by the fire, and I will make a bowl of rice for you and your canine companion. I would give you more, but it is all I have." Touched and amazed by the man's generosity, he thanked him. The friendly fellow prepared the rice, and the miser and his unnamed dog scarfed down the warm food and then fell asleep by the fire. When he awoke, he felt a joy in his heart that he had never felt. "Kind, compassionate man, you have shown me so much generosity and care. Would you please escort me home?" asked the miser. The poor cottage dweller was happy to oblige. Once home, the miserly man did something very uncharacteristic. He offered his newly acquired friend a luxurious room in his mansion and abundant amenities for life. His humble hero accepted his thoughtful gift, and over time the two formed a strong friendship. With each passing day, the miser's tight fist opened a little, allowing him to grow in understanding and generosity. He named his guard dog Pal and got to know and like his servants well. More importantly, anytime a beggar came to his door, he offered them a large bowl of warm rice and a comfortable bed in which to sleep.

In chapter 8 of *The Way of the Bodhisattva*, the wise and compassionate Indian Buddhist monk Shantideva wrote, "All the joy the world contains has come through wishing happiness for others. All the misery the world contains has come through wanting pleasure for oneself." If you are self-absorbed, you are cherishing yourself above others. To remedy this, you must vigilantly watch for any selfish motives. How many glances in the mirror do you take? Do you have all the answers? Is the biggest slice of pizza for you? How often do you post pictures of yourself? Is your suffering greater than that of everyone else? When the attitude of self-cherishing is strong, you're filled with thoughts of yourself and stand in your own way of happiness.

To transform something so insidious as self-cherishing, at the first sign of selfishness—when you are feeling GASSY—deal with the impulse immediately and directly. At first, it's challenging to sacrifice your narcissistic tendencies in any significant way. In small ways, sacrifice what benefits you for something that helps another. For example, when eating with others, if a bowl of fruit is set out and you decide to take the best piece, immediately see your self-cherishing attitude. Return the "best" piece of fruit or generously offer it to someone else. Think to yourself, "Self-cherishing has arisen in my mind. I must be cautious now." Catching your selfishness is crucial in all your practices.

To strengthen your healthy habit of thinking of others, try practicing the taking and giving meditation called *tonglen*. This practice uses your imagination and the yogic practice of breathing with alternating nostrils. Alternate nostril breathing induces relaxation and peace of mind. Begin by bringing to mind the suffering of someone you care for and imagine this person in front of you. Visualize breathing in their pain in the form of dark mist. Press on your right nostril and let this imagined mist enter your left nostril, move to your forehead, then down toward your heart center, where your self-cherishing dwells. Envision the dark mist rooting out your self-cherishing, so that understanding and compassion can grow within you. The dark mist then metamorphoses into a light-colored mist. Release your right nostril, then press down on your left. Envision the light-colored mist passing out of your right nostril and into your target audience, bringing them relief. Then repeat the process, breathing in through your right nostril and out through your left. Keep alternating nostrils, repeating the process for about ten to fifteen minutes. Visualize the person you care for relieved of what pains them.

In your day-to-day life, you can simplify this practice. Whenever you encounter someone suffering, breathe in their problem as dark mist, and breathe out the remedy as light mist. With regular tonglen practice, you'll see a definite change in your mind. Once you are good at taking and giving with loved ones, you can do it imagining conscious beings you feel neutral toward, like neighbors, stray animals, or store clerks. And once you get terrific at it, you can visualize people you dislike. However, that one may be far more challenging, even though it is vastly beneficial. Give it a try! I give you my guarantee that this practice will uproot your self-cherishing and increase your compassion.

# CHAPTER 6

# We Are All in This Together

THE FAMOUS mathematician and astronomer Nicolaus Copernicus is attributed with the saying, "To know that we know what we know, and to know that we do not know what we do not know, that is true knowledge." This father of modern astronomy was the one to point out that the earth revolves around the sun. If you're disappointed that the world doesn't revolve around you, you can take it up with Copernicus. Like so many other historic trailblazers, he was determined to discover the truth of the way things truly are. This inquiry into the truth starts with an idea to either prove or disprove some belief. Consider the notions about the earth that were prevalent before the time of Copernicus. In ancient times, there were many different ideas. Babylonians thought the earth's interior housed an underworld. Egyptians believed the world had four corners, like a cube, and mountains holding up the sky. It was the ancient Greeks that were certain the earth was round due to the spherical shape of the earth's shadow on the moon during an eclipse. This spherical hypothesis was periodically dismissed; in the sixth century Cosmas Indicopleustes, a Christian monk, referred to a description of the four corners of the earth in Revelations to support his claims of a flat earth. Even today there are some people that believe the earth is flat despite all the facts to the contrary. Ideally, people will reject unsubstantiated ideas and theories when there is no clear evidence or proof. Because if you have the right reason and accurate evidence, then unsubstantiated ideas can change. The Greek philosopher Aristotle saw for himself that the earth was spherical after watching ships gradually descend over the horizon; it was with his curiosity and the power of his observation that he was able to confirm the truth. You must be like Aristotle, curious to learn the truth, and like Copernicus, know what you know and admit to what you do not know.

The saying "ignorance is bliss" is a common expression. It implies that you are better off if you don't know the facts of a situation. But is *not* knowing really bliss? A long time ago in southern India, I was walking down a narrow alley with one of my students. We were completely engrossed in a conversation. Since it was a tight squeeze, we had to walk in single file. That didn't stop us from continuing to chat away. While moving briskly between two tall buildings, I realized my student had grown suspiciously quiet. Wondering why, I turned around to investigate. My student, who was far behind me, nervously pointed down at an irritable cobra coiled on the walkway between us. In southern India, there are a lot of cobras, so it is not that uncommon to encounter one slithering across your path. However, I was so immersed in the topic of our conversation that I didn't even see this venomous serpent as I walked by. My oblivion shocked me. I exclaimed, "Wow! There's a cobra! I didn't see it!" I was mere inches from being bitten by a big, venomous snake and didn't even know. The cobra was easily within striking range. My student smiled and shouted, "Ignorance is bliss, Rinpoche!" But if the cobra had bitten me, then ignorance would be suffering, not bliss at all! From then on, I've been more careful. Knowledge is excellent, but knowledge of your stupidity is wise.

A rainbow appears to be real, but it is an optical illusion. Catching a glimpse of this array of beautiful colors is dependent on various causes and conditions. A rainbow is dependent on things like water droplets and on where you are positioned in relation to the sun. This is one powerful way to demonstrate how your reality does not exist the way you perceive it. Perception and reality are two different things. Quantum physics can help us understand this. This branch of science is responsible for examining tiny objects, such as electron and proton particles. It is dedicated to studying energy and matter at its most basic level, with its aim to detect the behaviors and properties of nature's building blocks. Quantum phenomena exist all around you because everything is made up of particles and energy—even you! When you consider matter at this fundamental level, it changes your view.

## SEEING IS NOT BELIEVING

An atom was once understood as a particle that couldn't be divided anymore. The ancient Greeks were responsible for naming the atom, which means "not cuttable." But after investigation, we discovered that this name is a misnomer; atoms are made of smaller parts. The science behind the study of these miniscule parts is called particle physics. Since the discovery of the electron in the late nineteenth century, scientists went on to verify the existence of neutrons in the 1930s and revealed that the atom contains a central nucleus around 10,000 times smaller than the atom itself. In the 1960s, physicists then discovered something even smaller: quarks, which are the building blocks of protons and neutrons. They are believed to be 10,000 times smaller than protons and neutrons and the subatomic electron is speculated to be even smaller. Not even the most powerful particle accelerator can thoroughly investigate them.

While I personally haven't studied particle physics, as a philosophy teacher I do appreciate that this branch of science is revealing that things are not always what they seem. Even though quantum physicists have now divided material substances into extremely fine, subtle parts like quarks, they are currently technologically incapable of separating them further. At some point in the future, who knows what they will discover? You see, your perception of reality is like that, too. Things in your world just don't exist the way you think they do.

Not even your senses are trustworthy when it comes to seeing things accurately. Scholars claim that there is a disparity between how we see things and how things really are. Our senses are influenced by things such as self-preservation, strong memories, and imperceptible energies that cause us to see things incorrectly. Is it accurate to believe one hundred percent in our senses? People generally accept that whatever their eyes see, or their ears hear, matches entirely with their reality. However, you cannot place this kind of trust in your senses. According to the invisible gorilla experiment, performed by cognitive psychologists Daniel Simons and Christopher Chabris, our senses are unreliable. When people pay very close attention to one thing, they experience inattentional blindness—meaning they fail to notice other things, even if they are blatantly obvious.

Imagine you're at an event, like a football game, and you are highly engrossed in watching it. Then a person in a gorilla suit walks onto the field. You think you'd notice that, right? Incredible as it sounds, the gorilla experiment proved that there is a fifty percent chance you won't see the great ape at all! This is based on a selective attention experiment where participants watch people, half wearing white T-shirts and half black T-shirts, throw a ball around. The participants are tasked with counting the times those in white T-shirts pass the ball. Halfway through the experiment, a person in a gorilla suit walks into the middle of the game, pounds their chest, and then exits. Participants are then asked if they saw the gorilla. Over fifty percent do not. What's worse is they immediately fall into denial and claim they would have seen it if it were truly there! We can't always rely on our senses. I didn't see the cobra! So clearly, it's a challenge for us to know what we don't know.

Do you still think seeing is believing? Take another example: motion-induced blindness. That is when a small object, surrounded by a moving pattern, disappears from your sight and reappears a couple of seconds later. This occurs because the brain tends to discard information that it finds useless. Similar visual anomalies were found in 1976 by cognitive psychologists Harry McGurk and John MacDonald, who discovered that what a person hears is influenced by what they see. According to the McGurk effect, the brain can confuse watching the movement of someone's mouth and hearing what sounds the person is actually making. In the experiment, participants were asked to watch a video of a person saying "ba, ba, ba" with their eyes closed; in this case, participants correctly heard "ba, ba, ba." Then with the sound off but the video playing, some participants saw the person mouthing "ga, ga, ga." Then, with both sound and visuals playing, some participants reported hearing "da, da, da." Vision and hearing influence one another. Our most important sense organ, the brain, works hard to marry the sound with the visuals, but sometimes it has difficulty interpreting reality. Your senses are not always accurate.

There are hundreds of experiments that prove seeing is not believing. In 1889, German psychologist Franz Carl Müller-Lyer discovered that if two lines with arrowheads at their ends point in different directions, you'll see two different size lines—even though they are the same size. It doesn't stop there. Not even your sense of touch or taste is accurate. Metal, being a thermal conductor, will feel colder or warmer to the touch than a paper plate, even though they are the same temperature; even the color of a plate can alter what your food tastes like and the amount you would like to eat. Accordingly, you can see that your point of view is not as reliable as you think it is. Or maybe you have been reading so much that you have a reading-induced blindness and can't see that at all—a quip for those readers whose eyes may be tired.

## RELATIVE TRUTH, ULTIMATE TRUTH

Your sense organs go about constructing reality in a way that doesn't always reflect the truth. Buddhists believe that reality has two truths. We believe that there is a conventional truth and then the truth of connection; or, you could say, a relative truth, which is how we perceive this world, and an underlying truth. Relative truth pertains to our dualistic, or varied, way of thinking of phenomena, such as yourself, other beings, objects, emotions, and concepts. Absolute truth is the reality beyond this variable dualism and is the underlying nature of this relative world. These two truths exist side by side. As an example, when we look at the ocean, we see waves. A wave has a beginning, end, size, and shape, and as a result it seems solid and independent. When we deeply consider the wave, however, we discover that the cause of the wave is the vast ocean. The wave, being made of ocean, will ultimately dissolve back into the ocean. Both the wave and the ocean are truths; one relative and one ultimate, both the ocean. When we talk about the ultimate truth, we are talking about the cause or basis of something. What is ultimately true is that there is a unity to everything that tends do go undetected.

This underlying truth offers answers to the most profound questions, such as "Why is this water?" or "For what reason is one a person?" If I were to ask you, "Why is this water?" you would think that I'd gone entirely wacky! Yet if you truly understand the ultimate truth, you can answer that question. From the ultimate perspective, there is no water, because water is composed of a multifaceted unity. Like in quantum physics, the building blocks of water can be divided further and further down. It is a collection of particles that can be broken into hydrogen and oxygen, and even further divided into electrons, neutrons, and protons until there is no more water. Water does indeed exist as a useful form, a mental projection, and functional concept, but in reality, it is not the way you think it is. You could go as far as to say that water both exists and doesn't exist. But this is a little confusing, so instead just enjoy your refreshing glass of water that is also not water.

Can you see how this face-value relative truth and deeply considered ultimate truth might also be helpful in your personal life? It is conducive to know what type of problems you'll encounter when you don't know these two truths and what kind of benefits result from living with the knowledge of them. This is extremely important; suppose you cannot recognize and understand the conventional truth and the ultimate truth. In that case, you'll be more prone to profound mental and emotional suffering. Take, for example, a short-tempered person. When they get angry, they think the target of their rage exists precisely the same way that their distorted perception perceives them. They are looking only at the face-value truth. If that person said something harmful to this short-tempered individual, they see that person as harmful and nothing else. They don't consider the variety of factors that make up the big picture; they don't consider the underlying ultimate truth.

## CAUSES AND CONDITIONS

Anger arises from many different factors. Are you tired, or do you suffer from seasonal allergies? Either fatigue or allergies could cause you to feel particularly sensitive. Most people don't take all those sorts of factors into consideration. When they feel angry, they see only one predominant factor and isolate it from the other ones. That dominant factor overshadows the other factors, so it feels very independent, solid, and real. For example, suppose someone says something hurtful to you. It hurts your feelings, so you target that person and only feel angry at them, forgetting all the other circumstances that may have contributed to your anger. You develop a *blind* rage, so you can't see all the factors at play. This is not the case only with irritability. In this world, no matter what you engage in, you must consider the many different factors, causes, and conditions involved. Please try not to focus on one thing to hold independently accountable. Would you hold only your mouth responsible for eating the half-full bag of chips?

The truth is that things happen because other things contribute to them happening, resulting in an effect. Just like the ripple effect, actions have reactions. Since this is the truth, it means that all phenomena occur as a reaction to a prior cause. Then, in turn, the phenomenon conditions the results that follow. So the effect depends on the causes and conditions. One of my favorite books is Sun Tzu's *The Art of War*. It is the oldest known military treatise in the world. Chapter one starts with military general Sun Tzu naming off the conditions necessary for a successful battle. He says, "The art of war, then, is governed by five constant factors, to be taken into account in one's deliberations, when seeking to determine the conditions obtaining in the field. These are the moral law, heaven, earth, the commander, and the method and discipline." This shows General Tzu is thinking about the dependent factors, the conditions, necessary for successfully waging war. This truth of multi-factored dependency plays a significant role in war just as it does in peace building. To build peace, you need conditions such as truth, justice, and mercy.

## OUR SHARED DEPENDENCE

As the world grows more connected through globalization, our shared dependence on one another becomes even more visible. The COVID-19 pandemic kicked off a global supply chain issue that accentuated our worldwide dependency. Quite a few businesses temporarily closed at the height of the pandemic. This, among other COVID-19 mitigation strategies, resulted in a sharp decrease in the production and supply of goods; the entire economy was compromised, from manufacturing to shipping. Once everyone was ready to spend again and businesses began to reopen, the goods industry had changed in response to less demand. Worldwide shortages became commonplace, and price hikes were inevitable. Over many years, the world's countries have developed a clear multi-factored dependency on one another economically. If one country struggles, we all struggle, and you know the rest—when parts stop contributing to the whole, toilet paper goes missing from the shelves.

Everything is dependent on everything else, and parts rely on the whole. When energy and particles cooperate, individuals associate with one another, and nations cooperate, this collective interaction results in something emerging that is more phenomenal than the sum of the individual pieces. This is called emergence. An emergent property demonstrates the power of interdependence, of parts and components teaming up. What would happen if you were utterly solitary? When you think about it, your existence relies on things outside of yourself. You are not just you, but you are also everything! Bearing this in mind, our suffering and our joy is a team effort.

We are all in this together, and we are all of equal importance—no one is higher or lower, better or worse. Consider the computer. For a computer to function, it needs many different but essential parts. It needs things like screws, power cables, data cables, a motherboard, a screen, a keyboard, and so forth. These are all components. When you put all these things together, something emerges that is different and more powerful. Each piece becomes part of an incredible technological device that can do extraordinary tasks that the components are incapable of doing individually. The whole is greater than the sum of the pieces.

Let's look closely at a basic paperback. When analyzing a book, you can discern that it is made up of pages, and you know that these pages are made of paper, which comes from trees. We also know that the book has words printed in ink, as well as the glue or string that holds the pages together. There are also people such as the author and everyone who trained him, the editor and typesetter, the printer, truck driver . . . alas the list goes on! This book came about through the assemblage of numerous factors, or what you can call causes and conditions. It is easy to understand that all things arise from multiple causes and conditions when you consider what constitutes a book. When you see the big picture, you can realize that something so important as attaining happiness and eliminating suffering relies on more than just yourself alone.

Try to think of one particular thing that will make you happy all on its own. Is it a partner or wealth? I'd like you to know that relying on one thing to avoid suffering and be happy is a big mistake! For instance, many people find themselves single-mindedly engrossed in making money their whole lives. They believe that money will eliminate their hardships. But to have true happiness, you must really understand the many different factors that contribute to your life being a particular way and how you are reliant on the world around you. The life you're living is intimately entwined with everyone and everything. Your joy is contingent on the joy of others, and vice versa. Know you are unmistakably, indisputably, undoubtedly—to use the computer analogy—a part that works with other components to create something amazing. Knowing this, you have the precious knowledge that can lead to liberation.

Now that you understand how things indeed exist, you can work toward ending the suffering you feel. You have the key to the door that leads to reality, to the truth. Because you comprehend it, naturally, you can unlock the door and enter. But once inside, it is not enough to just know theoretically that we all exist interdependently;

this is a living knowledge. It only works if you apply it to your life. Engage in a practice that will help you investigate the many contributing factors to real solutions. A well-rounded approach considers others; it uses your wise mind and kind heart! Now you have opened the door to truth. You possess the precious knowledge of the truth of our interdependence, the insight that puts things into perspective.

# Reflection

Every year, deep in the forest, the oldest trees in an ancient grove discussed arboreal matters. One of the trees brought up how the animals in their forest were becoming more and more of a nuisance: "They disturb our roots, pick our leaves, break our branches, claw at our bark, and leave behind waste that smells horrendous!" Many of the trees felt the same. The entire tree grove agreed to figure out a way to rid themselves of these pesky animals. As they discussed these ideas, a large wildcat used the irritable tree as a scratching post. In response, it bent from side to side, making a loud creaking noise that scared the cat away. All the trees were amazed at how effective this method was, so the entire grove decided to do the same. Anytime an animal appeared, the trees would sway and creak to scare them away. Weeks passed, and before long, the entire grove was free of animals. "Finally!" they exclaimed. "We can live in peace!"

Because the grove was pest-free, the trees thought their problems were solved! But then the oldest trees heard a racket they had never heard before. A massive pack of curious animals was invading their grove. These odd animals were not as musical as the birds, as united as a pack of wolves, or as stealthy as the wildcats. One old tree overheard one of them shout out, "Timber!" Wherever these loggers went, they would make a loud clatter followed by an earth-shaking thud. These men showed no mercy and were not intimidated by the swaying of branches. The trees lamented getting rid of the animals with no wildcats to scare the men away. They realized how dependent on the forest's pesky beasts they indeed were.

* * *

In Buddhist traditions, emptiness is a key concept and closely related to interdependence. The emptiness of things refers to the understanding that everything in your world is composite and lacks a solid existence. This is absolute truth. This doesn't mean that things do not exist at all; distinctive things do appear to exist as individual phenomena, but only based on their relation to, or dependence on, other things. The two truths seem opposed and separate, but really, they are simply two aspects of one reality. This simply means that things do not exist in the way you perceive that they do. Ideally, it is best to consider both perspectives of reality; it is important that the appearance of separateness does not obscure the fact of our oneness. Like the trees in the ancient grove, you do not have an independent, irreducible self-nature. You share qualities with your civilization and culture, which is an assemblage of many historical factors. Furthermore, you are in a relationship with everyone and everything—and everyone and everything depends on something else for its existence. All your actions influence other lives, and vice versa. Within your constructed experience, the events that shape your life are from multiple causes and conditions. You can dissect anything into the components that make it up. Through analysis and careful introspection of your constituent parts, you will be able to see the patterns that have shaped your world. Discovering the reality of the way things are is critical to the development of wisdom and compassion.

The title "Rinpoche" is sometimes used to refer to an influential teacher in the Tibetan tradition. The term means "Precious Jewel" and often signifies that the teacher is a *tulku*, a recognized reincarnation of a prominent master. As a rinpoche, you do the same spiritual job lifetime after lifetime. Rinpoches are trained from childhood to help others. You spend your early years attending classes related to Buddhist study, practice, and ritual. Once your training is complete, you take over the responsibilities of your previous incarnations. This means taking on the task of helping those who suffer.

I am known as "Rinpoche." However, this recognition depends on many factors, causes, and conditions. I was a small child when the search party recognized me as a rinpoche. I needed to learn the word's meaning.

Slowly, because the people around me told me that as a rinpoche, I'm a particular person, I developed all kinds of different concepts regarding this label. I thought of myself as a special, important, unique, distinct individual. Eventually, I started to think that this was true! But when I tried to search for this rinpoche, asking, "Where is it? What is it?" I saw that there is nothing to be found. It was not something I had from the moment I was born; I only became a rinpoche when some people came and gave me that title and responsibility to be of spiritual service to others.

Being a rinpoche is something that relies on so many different things. You are just like me in that way. Take time to reflect on all the conditioned factors that have shaped your identity and then meditate on the emptiness of your self-concept. Consider how you have been conditioned over your lifetime to see yourself a certain way and how you have labeled yourself "me" based on these particular attributes. Briefly ponder the formation of your personal identity, from your earliest memory until now. Then attempt to find this "me" within yourself. Try to find it in your physical form. Is it in your body? Where? Then try to find the "me" in your sense perception. Are you in what you are feeling, hearing, seeing, smelling, or tasting? Next consider whether the "me" is in your perception of what you are sensing or recognizing. Are you in the objects you perceive? Then ponder whether the "me" is within your mental formations like your thoughts, beliefs, or reactions. Are "you" in your thoughts, as a solid entity? Lastly reflect on whether the "me" is in your conscious awareness. Is the "me" within the awareness that you exist? Ask yourself, If the "me" is not there, where could it be? It is okay to feel initially frightened or confused if you do not find yourself. The realization of your emptiness can feel like losing a precious item. However, once you acquire a deep understanding of the wisdom of emptiness coupled with its opposite, the relative truth, you can become spiritually balanced and find true equanimity.

# CHAPTER 7

# Transforming Sand into Pearls

W HEN YOU are equipped with the truth, the world is your oyster! Not just any mollusk, but a home for precious pearls. You've walked through the door of reality to experience what this fantastic world of insight offers. But you find no one is entitled to happiness—rather, it is developed through integrating practice into your life and the positive change this brings. Authentic mind training practice is not passive; it is something that you mentally cultivate to be able to apply it to the obstacles you face in daily life. Just as the oyster creates a pearl in response to the irritation of sand. It is worth mentioning that there are many spiritual practices that have a similar aim. For example, some Buddhist traditions use chanting or devotional practices to this end. But the type of training that I am asking you to do, both at the end of each of these chapters and the end of the book, are contemplative practices. Contemplative practices have been at the center of many philosophical, humanistic, and religious traditions since antiquity. Christian, Jewish, Hindu, Muslim, pagan, and other traditions have well-developed contemplative practices. Then there are some nonreligious contemplative practices within the mindfulness movement, which focus primarily on calming yourself. The mind training practices you'll be asked to do here do not require you to be religious, nor are they just about being calm or stress-free. Even though they are a version of the core mind training practice found in all lineages of Tibetan Buddhism, they are intended here to be secular. They're for everyone who just wants to stop suffering and have some solid, lasting happiness. You do this by directing your mind and heart toward what is wholesome. But before you train your mind, you must trust in your ability to be awake to the obstacles to practice. Use them like the oyster uses grit to make pearls. Inspiring an atmosphere of practice through patience, perseverance, and determination to stay the course is vital to your success.

## THE OUTER OBSTACLE

Everyone has hoops to jump through if they want to achieve something. But it is important to see that obstacles don't block your way— they point out a better way. For actual mind training practice, you must use your obstacles as a means to practice. When you look at it that way, obstacles are helpful. There are three types of obstacles that I am sure many of us can practice with. The first is the outer obstacle. These are obstacles that appear to manifest from outside of us, such as a smartphone. An outer obstacle can be as simple as habitually checking the social media feed on your phone or binge-watching your favorite show rather than committing yourself to using your time constructively. In this case, your practice is pushing the off button.

Some obstacles don't have an off button. School, family, friends, or your place of employment are button-free. For example, I have a student who is a fashion designer, who interacts with models and other fashion industry professionals. It is challenging for her to incorporate mind training into her work setting, where the expectation is that she dress and behave fashionably, not wisely. Although fashion can be a creative expression, the industry routinely promotes a GASSY lifestyle that motivates people to critique and judge others' appearances. Such comparison is an obstacle to finding true happiness. Comparing is divisive and encourages you to focus your attention outward. You then spend your time considering how your appearance and social status sizes up to the competition. How would you feel if you purchased a new outfit and wore it for three days straight—would you feel uncomfortable wearing it more than once? You probably do not wear the same clothes repeatedly out of concern for harsh judgment. That is because there is social pressure to look smart. According to a study led by Princeton University, people make split-second decisions on someone's competency based solely on what they are wearing. Those wearing more expensive-looking clothing were deemed more competent than persons in "poorer" attire. It makes me wonder what a monk or nun's competency rating would be. For Buddhist monastics, we have no choice; we must shave our heads and wear the same modest clothes day after day. A Buddhist monk or nun makes the choice to live a simple lifestyle. When we shave our heads and wear basic clothing, we are following in the footsteps of the Buddha and showing our commitment to the pursuit of enlightenment and helping others. It is a symbol of giving up the worldly attachments that keep people from true happiness. We are okay doing that. In fact, we never have a bad hair day!

If you're not a monastic, it's easy to feel peer pressure to wear something sharp and different from the day before. This may be emphasized more in highly competitive societies. This type of outside obstacle is something you must be conscious of and work with. Ideally, you need to find people who support your inner growth and transformation. Otherwise, you need a very secure self-belief to challenge this obstacle. No matter what, overcoming your fixation with what is exterior and instead moving your focus inside yourself, to generate self-knowledge and inner strength, is something you must practice in order to be genuinely happy.

## THE INNER OBSTACLE

The bright side is that all obstacles provide an excellent opportunity for self-improvement. You will learn some obstacle-removing practices at the end of this chapter that you can put to use. For now, though, let's consider the second obstacle: the inner obstacle. Inner obstacles are caused when you're feeling physically unwell. When you struggle with issues pertaining to health and wellness, feelings of discomfort can be distracting to training your mind. When you have this obstacle, it is essential to assess whether you are living a lifestyle that encourages well-being. If not, show yourself some compassion and engage in self-care. And when you do train your mind, practice within your physical limits. If you're still unable to work with your inner obstacles or practice well, seek out a qualified teacher or physician, depending on your circumstance.

For instance, once there was this person who had such an inner obstacle, but still wished to learn to practice training their mind, so they went to a mind training teacher. Despite wanting to practice, their exhaustion always got in the way. After some assessment, it was discovered that they enjoyed eating big meals prior to engaging in mind training. Since their body was spending so much energy digesting their food, they had difficulty concentrating on the teachings, practices, or anything. The teacher saw this person's dilemma, so simply said to them, "The person who does not eat heavy or does not eat light will train great and be the happiest." Thanks to this teaching the student realized the value of moderation. When you set out to do such training, it is very helpful to live balanced between extremes. If you are suffering health-wise with an issue unrelated to balance, like cancer or a disability, mind training practice can always be adjusted, regardless of what ails you. The important thing is to respect your limitations but not give up your practice.

## THE SECRET OBSTACLE

The last obstacle is called a secret obstacle. Secret obstacles are more like negative habits that are deeply ingrained and perhaps go without our notice, such as procrastination. Procrastination is one of the worst and most insidious obstacles of all. The Latin root for this term is *procastinatus*, where *pro* means forward and *crastinus* means tomorrow. You put off what you could do today for tomorrow. There are a lot of factors that contribute to developing this bad habit, but it all comes down to attachment. You may be attached to your sofa and be a couch potato. If that is the case, you can practice where you have planted yourself. You may be attached to a perfect outcome, so you don't even try. You might be attached to fleeting pleasures, so you put off what is less pleasurable. You may be attached to seeking joy, and don't have time because you run from one thing to another seeking satisfaction. You may be attached to safety, so you put off what you fear until tomorrow. Does your tomorrow ever come?

A simple example of the problem with attachment can be found in the story of the fearful elephant. Once there was a young, white elephant that lived free and happy in the forest. One day a king passed by and couldn't resist capturing such a unique and amazing beast. The king ordered that the elephant be kept in a pen and prodded until it was broken and ready to ride. The noise of all this prodding terrified the timid, gentle elephant so much that he broke the pen in terror and ran for the forest. The king's men couldn't find the elephant, but this didn't stop it from being terrified of the slightest noise. For weeks, a crinkle of a leaf, the sound of the wind, and even the tiniest click of a beetle sent the elephant flying into a panic. Seeing this, an owl felt compassion and decided to help. She flew down and said, "Please don't be afraid, I'm just a small bird that means you no harm. You needn't fear me, the trees, the wind, or the beetles. You are the greatest beast for miles. The king's men are not here, but the fear you created is—and it is controlling you. You can end your unhealthy attachment to safety, but you must train your mind to challenge your fears." The elephant thanked the owl and from that day forward began to work at controlling his fears. Anytime he heard a sound, he reminded himself not to be afraid. He stopped himself from bolting to safety and instead investigated where the noise was coming from. Over time, he conquered his fear.

Breaking your unhealthy habits in order to develop continuity in your practice starts with understanding the cause of your obstacle. It can begin with a simple question that helps you see where you are getting stuck. What are you attached to?

## BREAKING HABITS

There is a comic strip about an imaginative little boy named Calvin and his best friend Hobbes, a toy tiger. The little boy imagines his stuffed tiger to be real. In one of the comics, the boy and his parents are gone for the entire day. No one is there to feed his voracious tiger at his normal time. Because he is so attached to himself, the boy starts thinking of his safety upon his return home. He surmises, "If my parents go in first, I'm safe. However, if I enter the house first, my hungry tiger will pounce on me and scarf me down!" I told this story to a young student at Sera Jey who was attached to snacking—somewhat like the imaginary tiger. I showed him the comic strip and asked him, "Do you ever get this hungry for snacks?" He told me that he did, so I asked him what kind of foods he daydreamed about. He said to me that he frequently daydreamed about eating a wide variety of delicious snack foods. This is how each person's mind works—if you think of and then do something repeatedly, you'll subconsciously think of and do that thing repeatedly.

The same is true of mind training practice. If you keep practicing, it eventually becomes a healthy habit. Therefore, you must develop a habit of directing your mind toward what is wholesome in order to strengthen it. Mind training practice is not just sitting there silently with a blank mind. Mind training is about overcoming obstacles, developing healthy mental habits, and emotional strength training, all of which lead to positive mental states. The important thing in your mind training practice is not to develop the habit of avoidance. To prevent this, you may find you need to practice little by little, but don't give up. At the end of this book there is a series of mind training practices; make a commitment to follow them for a solid month. If training goes well, keep it up. Don't let the three obstacles get in your way to living a life that will be of benefit to others and to yourself.

## BUILDING YOUR ENDURANCE

Training your mind takes endurance. Most of us want immediate results in our lives in place of hard work. This practice is like training for a marathon. You first run one mile, then gradually build your stamina until you reach twenty-six miles. And you have to be consistent with your training. That way, when it is time to run the twenty-six miles, you won't poop out. We must have the common sense not to expect immediate results. Looking for shortcuts fosters impatience. More importantly, the search for a shortcut undermines our capability to work hard. The reality is we live in a world of timesavers. In the twenty-first century, everything has become instant and fast: instant noodles, instant oatmeal, frozen prepackaged meals, fast coffee, fast food, fast and instant everything. But there is no such thing as an instant pearl. If you want the pearls of happiness, you must be patient and cultivate your endurance.

## PATIENCE

Part of endurance entails being able to undergo difficulties and suffering. Some people will give up once they encounter the tiniest of sufferings. As soon as they face some problem, they want to throw in the towel. This happens because they have the mistaken idea that this world is a happy, faultless place. But this is not heaven. If it were heaven, then going to the dentist wouldn't be such a painful experience, and there would be an endless supply of toilet paper. No, life is more like an adventure! Even so, as soon as you encounter some minor problem, you find it so difficult to bear, lose hope, then stop practicing. Don't stop—accept that there is a lot of suffering and hardship in the world and find serenity in it by continuing your efforts to shape a positive mindset. Adopt a problem-solving attitude and never shy away from difficulties. Use your practice to deal with issues that arise as best as you possibly can. When you are mentally inclined to face challenges and use your mind training practices, the suffering you experience weakens. Therefore it is necessary to willingly face obstacles and undertake hardships. Life's inevitable challenges offer you an opportunity to use your mind-training skills and strengthen your resolve. The development of endurance and consistency in your practice is enough; you needn't focus on the results.

On the other hand, you may set your expectations too high; this can lead to impatience and then giving up. Be patient with your training. Be like a tortoise: slow and steady. If you want results, you must work hard. Be patient and shift your focus from those lofty expectations to rolling up your sleeves. Challenge your desire for quick results, your impulse to want instant pearls. For instance, let's say you go into a bookstore. You see one book with the title *How to Become Rich Overnight!* and another book entitled *How to Become Rich in Ten Years!* Which book would you choose? I, for one, would pick the book that promises riches in one night! Just like everyone else, my mind is impulsive and selfish by nature. This is one of the reasons why people play the lottery, even though the chances of winning are not in your favor. J. P. Morgan, a statistics professor at Virginia Tech, offers a comparison to help clarify the likelihood of someone winning a Mega Millions jackpot. Suppose it takes a minute for you to complete a Mega Millions entry form and pay for it. If you do this every minute, nonstop, it would take you 575 years to enter all possible combinations. Now consider the likelihood of you having the winning combination. Knowing there is a minuscule chance of becoming rich overnight, many people still take that chance. Fortunately, a significant portion of the money people spend on lottery tickets goes to support worthy causes, such as senior support agencies, homeless shelters, and public schools. If you are interested in making a profit, however, it's better to go the old-fashioned route and save your money. Who knows how much you could amass? Keep this in mind and expect similar results from your practice. Ground yourself in reality and practice by degrees. Results from practice do not come overnight, but over time. If you apply patience and perseverance to your practice, who knows how much insight you can amass?

I learned the value of patience early. When I was a young monk, I asked my superior, "How long will it take a person to master this practice?" He replied, "It will take one million years for anyone to master it." Astounded and baffled by how much time it would take, I thought to myself, "Well, this is not the job for me! This will take way too long!" Now I realize that my superior was trying to teach me a lesson in patience. When you can be patient and work hard, the results will come naturally to you. I am so grateful for his encouragement.

What a tremendous benefit it is to have the support of like-minded people.

The company you keep will help you cultivate patience or hinder it. If you're around impatient people who want speedy results and not hard work, it will rub off on you. On the flip side, if you value a supportive environment and surround yourself with others who respect hard work, they will help you foster your endurance. If you can't find people of the same mind, you'll have to rely on your own strong self-belief. That is why you must cultivate a powerful trust in yourself, which can be very challenging to do. Perhaps you've become suspicious of your ability to handle difficulties, or perhaps you are anxious about life or don't really trust your inner compass. Training your mind will build your self-trust.

## LIKE A DELICIOUS POT OF TEA

Developing self-belief through mind training is like developing the ability to make a delicious pot of tea from scratch. First you generate the motivation—you must have the desire to enjoy a pot of tasty tea. Having desire is skillful in this circumstance, when you are directing it toward something positive. That way you'll feel motivated. Then generate the thought that you are capable of learning how to make marvelous tea. Even if you don't believe it fully, you should at least think encouraging thoughts by telling yourself that you're able. When you feel inclined to begin the process, you boil the water, measure a certain amount of tea leaves, steep it for a considered amount of time, then pour it into the right vessel. The next step is very important: don't be attached to the results. If the tea tastes bad, resist discouragement and analyze any mistakes you've made, then reapproach your method. You can try things like steeping it at a different temperature or changing the amount of tea you use. Keep trying until you have the right outcome. What you are developing is knowledge of how to make delicious tea. It's important to analyze outcomes so you can correct any errors, make better batches, and generate enthusiasm toward future improvements. The development of self-improvement is similar. First you have the desire for improvement, then you develop self-knowledge. Generating self-knowledge starts with using ingredients such as the precious knowledge of the truth, the nature of your mind, and the methods to train it. As you practice mind training, you look at things like how the mind works and what it takes to make improvements. As you move through the mind training procedure, if you find that your mind is not improving, analyze what you may be doing wrong, then reapproach your method. Don't give up! Stay unattached to the outcome. Just as you must be aware of the different ingredients and procedures to make delicious tea, you must also be mindfully aware of your thoughts, words, and actions for clues on what needs changing in order to develop beneficial qualities.

You are your own teacher and your own pupil in the school of life. If you follow the delicious tea method to train your mind, you'll mature as a person and encourage a solid faith in your thoughts and behavior. No practice will bring about the desired results unless you undertake it with the proper frame of mind: a mind that is open and interested in improvement. This openness is a wonderful kind of magic that is available to each of us. When you are genuinely willing to change what your mind focuses on, it is possible to successfully adopt a healthy approach to life. In fact, everyone has the capability to live well. Making changes in your life depends upon hope— upon the sincere wish for self-improvement. You need hope and the determination it brings because, essentially, only you can help yourself. You are your own hero, so face your problems with courage. Be mindful of your troublesome issues; that way you can precisely identify the causes of those problems and fix them.

When you encounter difficulty in mind training, consider the nature of the problem and then determine its cause. Upon reflection, you may find it more than likely that you have been reacting to challenges by complaining and protesting rather than deciding to handle them head-on. Such reactivity is not helpful to you, but since your mind has struggled with negativity for so long, using mind training to suddenly force it in another direction is extremely difficult!

For example, say a person goes to a teacher and asks for a helpful practice. The teacher tells this person, "Practice is very easy. All you need to do is sit down, close your eyes, and focus on the value of compassion. But whatever you do, do not think of a monkey!" Your first response is, "Oh, this is easy," and then you go home to practice. Once home, you sit comfortably, and focus your mind on the value of compassion. It goes great for a minute or two, but then your mind quickly switches to thoughts of the monkey. Pretty soon, all you can think about is the monkey! Where did your focus on compassion go?

This is like social psychologist Daniel Wegner's well-known thought suppression experiment. He asked test subjects to verbalize their stream of consciousness for five minutes. Then, they were instructed not to think of a white bear. If they did, they'd have to ring a bell. Needless to say, they rang the bell frequently! The subjects were unable to suppress the thought of the white bear. Another group was told it was okay to think of a white bear, and they didn't ring the bell as often. This is just how problematic your mind can be. It can be challenging to practice; thus, you must be patient with yourself. Otherwise, you might just spend your time suppressing thoughts. Training your mind is not thought suppression, it is thought strengthening. It is choosing to give attention to what is true and what is healthy. You learn to be conscious of things like compassion and at the same time let go of unhelpful thoughts about monkeys or bears. This is important because it helps you build self-belief, as well as the wise mind and kind heart necessary to live happily.

## TRUE HAPPINESS COMES FROM THE INSIDE

You've read this far, so now you know: nothing is permanent; GAS is a big problem; hope is essential; we are in this together; and nothing is as it seems. You need to overcome obstacles to training your mind, believe in your abilities, and apply patience and determination. But all these words amount to a hill of beans if you don't put them to use. These words are part of a living knowledge and living practice— essential for living a happy life! It's not uncommon for people to look for happiness outside themselves, by listening to music, watching films, surfing the net, and scrolling through their social media feed. But in my experience, the kind of happiness that self-knowledge and mind training provide is far superior. I've never used a smartphone, and my daily expenses are minimal, but I'm very happy!

Finding happiness is tricky in the digital age. When I was a teacher at the university, I'd encounter students who were habitually attached to their devices. For instance, Sera Jey Monastic University is part of a student exchange program with a private American college. While we were arranging the curriculum, one of the American professors who helped organize the exchange emphasized that their students would be reasonably flexible about food and accommodation, but not about technology. She said that they'd definitely need internet access because the internet is "in their blood." This seems to be the case with most of the younger generation. One time, while on a retreat in India, one of the participants told me that when they sat down for an hour-long practice session, they switched their phone to mute and placed it next to their seat. But afterward, they admitted that they couldn't stop wondering if they were missing a call or text. It made it impossible for them to concentrate.

I do understand that in this digital age, people are reliant on their mobile phones for things like work or staying in touch with family and friends. This is nothing to fret about. However, problems arise when people become addicted to their cell phones. A 2018 Pew Research Center survey by analyst Jingjing Jiang concluded that nearly fifty-five percent of teens in the United States profess to be addicted to their smartphones. What's more, thirty-five percent of teens use their phones while driving, forty-five percent believe that their phone is their most valuable possession, and forty-eight percent feel anxiety when their battery goes below the twenty percent mark. This suggests that the phone is no longer merely a tool for communication; it is an obsession. It is something people are attached to in the hopes that it will bring them satisfaction. I suspect that things like the internet, social media, and memes factor into this addiction.

TRANSFORMING SAND INTO PEARLS    115

However, much people rely on external things for their happiness, they won't find satisfaction through these devices.

True happiness happens on the inside, when we train our minds to accept the truth and respond to this truth in a healthy way. This training doesn't mean becoming superhuman. It means you believe in yourself enough to have faith in your abilities to transform for the better. You build confidence when you know how to function well in this web of dependency. You are a person who wants real, genuine happiness. We all want that! Even though the world is your oyster, you are the one who is actually responsible for making the pearls. You are in charge of generating your own joy. In doing so, you will influence those around you in a good way. Mind training practice is a tool to overcome problems and ineffective habitual tendencies. It's a way to happiness. It doesn't have anything to do with your outer circumstances; it is a matter of your inner freedom and purity. It's a way of conquering the problematic tendencies and conditioning embedded in your mind.

## TRANSFORM PROBLEMS INTO PEARLS

You must decrease the frequency of your negative tendencies so that you can transcend them. Until you find a way to overcome internal problems, they will always be with you, causing a host of avoidable problems that leave you in misery. This is an eternal truth, not something that I invented. I'm merely pointing it out to you so that I can help you discover happiness and true freedom through practice. It is not enough to have a simple intellectual understanding of how to overcome your negative tendencies. No matter how well you understand these teachings theoretically, it will not do you any good if you do not apply them to your life. As I said, they will amount to a hill of beans. It's unnecessary to have extensive knowledge; if you simply know how to practice correctly, you will gain plenty of benefits. Even if you deeply understand profound philosophical topics, you will miss the mark if you do not know how to apply any of it to solve your daily problems. You must use what you have learned to train not only your mind but also your heart. The kind heart and the wise mind are connected. They are in cahoots! Therefore, your mind and heart have a significant impact on one another. Perhaps that is why the medical community has linked depression with cardiovascular disease. The mind and heart are like two wings of a bird. You cannot fly with only one wing. You only soar when both wings work together.

Working with your mind and heart is something you must do for yourself; no one can do it for you. Now's the time to make a vow to practice and follow through. Once you have set your practice goal, you must resolutely strive to reach it. You'll never get anywhere if you don't know what your intentions are or if you continually delay practicing. Inner transformation begins with deciding, finally, to act. You needn't be overly strict with yourself—after all, you are only human. Essentially, there is no right or wrong way to engage in the practice. The most important thing is that you are making an effort. Don't get hung up on doing things perfectly—just keep going. Rather, as your practice matures, it is crucial to investigate whether it's helping you or not. Use the delicious tea method. Periodically reflect on whether your negative tendencies have decreased or not. If you find that it is working, then keep practicing! The most important thing is to benefit from using this information and to engage in practice. If your efforts are sincere, your life and the lives of those around you will benefit. If you do not get a satisfactory result, it's time for you to consider a different approach.

From this moment forward, consider the knowledge I've shared with you and the mind training practices as something like taking a new medicine for what ails you. When taking this powerful medication, take it in small doses and then spend some time reflecting on how it's affecting you and your life. If you feel you're improving, keep taking the medicine as usual. Use the mind training techniques you learn in this book as an antidote to what troubles you. Use them at every opportunity. If you form this habit, at the first sight of trouble, you'll spontaneously apply the correct antidote. And once you form the good habit of practicing, it's important to occasionally make a follow-up appointment with yourself. Set aside time to reflect on whether your world is improving. The most important thing is that through your practice, you become healthier and happier.

Sand irritates an oyster, and the oyster responds by making a beautiful pearl. Transformation happens through difficulties. Your daily life is filled with challenges, but these problems needn't cause you misery. You needn't fear your troubles; they are a means to grow and learn. If you encounter obstacles, see them as an opportunity to practice taking control of your mind. There is powerful medicine in knowing the truth and engaging in mind training practice. With precious insight, self-belief, hope, endurance, and a strong determination, the world is your oyster. But it is up to you to transform your problems into pearls.

# Reflection

A winded fox, fleeing hunters, came across a logger about ready to chop down a tree. Fearing for his life, the fox begged and pleaded for the forester to help him find a good hiding place. The logger was not the sort to help others, but since the fox wouldn't let up, he agreed to hide the restless little creature in his nearby cabin. The woodsman opened the door to his dwelling, allowing the fox to quickly creep inside and hide while the man remained outside. Shortly after he closed the door, a group of enthusiastic hunters arrived with their barrage of restless hounds. "Hello, woodsman! Did you happen to see a fox pass by?" asked one of the huntsmen. "Oh no, I definitely did not see a fox!" shouted the logger while gesturing wildly that the fox was in his home. The hunters thought the man's gestures were odd and unrelated to his words, so they thanked him and went about their way. Once the hunters were gone, the fox raced for the open door. "Hey, aren't you going to thank me for saving your life?" asked the logger. The fox turned around and replied sternly,

"I would have thanked you, but since actions speak louder than words, I now know the truth about how you feel." With that said, the fox bolted back into the shadows of the forest.

Our words and actions should match. The position, or view, that lies behind any philosophical or religious doctrine is similar to playing with words. A philosophical view is essentially a search for a truth, or an insight, that is regarded very highly. But spiritual wisdom is incomplete when it is merely based on words. Of course, for your practice to go well, you must know about all this philosophical information. However, you find wisdom through analyzing deep concepts, and also through meditation or mind training practice. You can't develop faith without discovering the truth of the way things are, so analysis and meditation are essential. However, all the explanations and debates to find out what is true are the equivalent of playing word games. You don't want to get caught up in words. All this analysis and investigation must have a limit, or you can't progress. That is why once you realize the truth about things, you must put words into action by applying this insight to your life.

It's crucial to explore the relationship between what you have learned, your practice, and how well it works in your life. In short, you need to consider the proper balance between knowledge and practice, with the ultimate priority given to putting what you learn to use daily. Consider your obstacles. Obstacles are valuable because they can be the starting point to help you move beyond words, into the realm of action. In my Buddhist tradition, there is an excellent contemplative form of mind training passed down from the Indian sage Atisha called the *Seven Points of Mind Training*. Later masters expanded these points into a series of profound slogans that the practitioner must contemplate to generate wisdom and compassion; one of these slogans helpfully suggests that you work with your greatest obstacle first. This chapter discussed the three obstacles: outer, inner, and secret. Consider which one of the three is the most significant block to your positive transformation. Sometimes there is more than one, but start with the most obvious first. Be honest and resist going into denial.

Once you find your most significant obstacle, consider the root cause. Ask yourself in what way you are responsible for this obstacle. Is it related to an attachment, self-cherishing, or GAS? After you understand what needs to change and why, incorporate that into your practice. Based on your greatest obstacle, your practice could be as basic as a calm abiding meditation, where you settle the mind through mental concentration on a particular object, such as the breath; or it could be a more mentally engaged, analytical meditation where you deeply consider a particular topic, exploring it from every angle to gain insight. These two types of meditation are also helpful when used together. Calm abiding helps prime your mind prior to analysis. That way you are less distracted and able to achieve greater insight. Keep track of your progress by writing down the obstacle, a small manageable goal, and a time by which you think you can reasonably meet that goal. Chart your daily progress by writing the number of minutes you practice on a calendar. Here are some examples using the three obstacles.

*Outer Obstacle*: The obstacle is the lack of spiritual support in your environment, which dissuades you from practicing. Self-belief can help you develop determination to keep you on the spiritual path. Your goal is to do analytical meditation for ten minutes each day upon waking. Focus on developing a solid sense of self-belief by analyzing why you are valuable in this interdependent world. You'd like to make it a habit by X weeks.

*Inner Obstacle*: The obstacle is poor sleep hygiene due to a restless mind. Your goal is to practice ten minutes of shamatha, or calm abiding meditation, before bedtime. Use your breath as your focal point. When your mind wanders, return to counting the breath. You'd like to make this a habit by X weeks.

*Secret Obstacle*: The obstacle is procrastination. Your goal is to practice five minutes of focusing on your breath and five minutes of analytical meditation on impermanence. You'd like to make this a habit by X weeks.

Habits are actions triggered automatically. According to a habit formation study in *The British Journal of General Practice*, habits form when coupled with something you already do. An example of good habit formation is doing meditation upon waking in the morning. The signal to meditate is waking up, then you repeat this same action consistently in the same context. The myth is that it takes twenty-one days to form a habit, but everyone is different. Research suggests that the average time it takes to form a habit is sixty-six days. That is why you want to keep practicing for at least ten weeks. If you find in the last week of tracking that you've generated a solid, healthy habit, it's cause for a real celebration!

# CHAPTER 8

# Mind Nesting and Thought Resting

As I HAVE mentioned previously, when I was young, various factors led to me having ornithophobia, an irrational fear of birds. Typically, this originates from negative encounters with real or imagined birds in childhood. There are quite a few people who have had unpleasant encounters with these feathered creatures and consequentially have developed this phobia. Did you know that pigeons and gulls are the most likely culprits to induce such dread? So many people enjoy feeding pigeons and seaside gulls, so there is little wonder that this innocuous enjoyment can turn unpleasant after one unexpected peck on your toe.

Abnormal fears often result from normal life events. Tons of people suffer from anxiety-provoking phobias; in the United Kingdom alone, it is estimated that approximately ten million people live with phobias. But where do these fears come from? My apprehension of birds is inside my mind as a thought. It's good to know that it's the *thought* that is causing the problem, not the bird itself. Birds won't actually start swooping down from the sky and attacking me! When I think of it, thoughts are like our feathered friends. Inside your conscious mind, thoughts fly around like wild birds. They fly in the sky of your awareness. Your mind watches thoughts flutter from subject to subject like the sky watches birds fly from tree to tree. But if you build a nest, you put your troublesome thoughts to rest. You build this nest by applying the *tweetment*. (I can't resist a corny pun.) You train your mind.

After gradually working with the fear in my mind, I am happy to report that I am ninety percent less afraid of birds. This is because we hold sway over our powerful mind. This thing that we call "mind" is boundless energy that cannot be destroyed. The mind is a continuum that is never broken but endlessly undergoes various transformations. This is encouraging news, because it means you are not stuck in your fears, or anything else. You can generate positive transformation through mind training practice. Your mind is essentially unstoppable, infinite. It is the root of all experiences and the foundation of happiness and suffering. Therefore, it is purely through training the mind that you attain peace and happiness. And mind training is not emptying your mind of thoughts, as some may assume all meditation practices to be. It is training your mind to focus on specific healthy, transformative thoughts, until functional thinking becomes automatic.

## WHAT IS IT THAT YOU ARE TRAINING?

By training your mind, you can put your burdensome thoughts at rest. But before you can put them to rest, you must first find your mind. I recall one famous story about a great master of mind training and a student who looked for his mind. In this story, a very determined student sought an excellent mind-training master in the hopes he would teach him. Initially, the master ignored him, but the student stood in the freezing, cold snow until he was waist-deep to show his commitment. The master thought the student was shallow and self-centered. But the student dared to offer the master his arm as a symbol of his true desire for instruction in mind training. Seeing the student's commitment to learning, he agreed to teach him. The student then asked, "Master, I cannot feel joy because I'm overwhelmed with anxious thoughts. Will you help me to soothe my mind?" The master insightfully asked his student, "Can you give me your mind? If you can give me your mind, I will soothe it." Then, the student looked for his mind everywhere. Bewildered, he replied, "Although I sought it, I cannot find my mind." The master revealingly replied, "There! I have now soothed your mind." The master had disclosed the truth of the student's mind: its primordial and empty essence, or selflessness. Like the state of matter, all things disappear when their particles are divided down. It's the same with thoughts. When thoughts are divided down and you look for your mind, it is not there. Your mind cannot be objectified because there is nothing tangible to grasp. The mind's mental energy has the nature of awareness, clarity, and knowing. So what is it that you are training?

Let me be clear. Even though you can't find your mind, it doesn't mean that you do not have influence over its energy. Thoughts, choices, and emotions work together to impact this energetic force. Analytical mind training helps you to not grasp at negative thoughts, to direct your attention toward wholesome thoughts, to make more functional choices, and, as a result, to experience preferable emotions. The advantages do not end there. Your mental energy affects the physical world, in particular, your physical body. The particles that make up your physical form and the energy of your mind are intimately connected, such that when you train your mind, you directly impact the health of your brain, the well-being of your body, and even influence the interconnected world around you. Later, we'll probe these ideas, but before we do, you first must wonder how your mind got so far off track.

When you take a moment to explore your inner world, isn't it peculiar that you can effortlessly feel your negative emotions, but you cannot find your mind? What causes your distress is inside of your awareness, but it's not the mental energy itself, it is a habitual grasping at negativity. It is important to uncover the root cause of all these negative emotions. When you begin your inner exploration, do you ask, are these emotions I am clinging to coming from myself? Who is this "self"? This inquiry brings you closer to the truth of who you really are and how you developed a negativity bias. When you search, you become aware that there are a lot of factors over the course of your lifetime that have influenced you to be a certain way. You have been deeply conditioned by various memories. It dawns on you how the outside world contributed to building the self. In my case, I have the title "Rinpoche," so that has played into my self-concept. Your encounters with the world may have you believing certain things about yourself, too. There are a lot of causes and conditions that have shaped this relative self. This sort of small self is impermanent and changeable. Upon deeper investigation, the more you begin to clear away your self-concepts, the more you clear ineffectual imprints from your mind. Then, it's like the light of wisdom comes on, and you can see the truth. That you are the result of this connection to everyone and everything. This allows you to perceive selflessness and experience some relief from grasping at negative emotions.

You are mightier than you know! From the moment you break your old self-concepts, you witness the truth of how you are interconnected with the world around you. Your relationship to everything around you transforms when you experience selflessness, because your relationship with yourself changes. Your surroundings will physically appear the same. However, once you truly realize that you are part of everything, you stop all the selfish, negative rumination. When you surrender your limited self and accept the deeper wisdom of the truth, you feel linked to something astoundingly limitless. Like a wave in the ocean, you are subject to all the changes a wave undergoes, yet you can't deny that you're made of the wide expanse of the mighty ocean.

Can you imagine how much your self-belief would increase if you fully recognized the limitless nature of your own interconnected being? That is why understanding your connection to everything is so crucial to ending your suffering. It helps you see the problem with your self-centered fixation, but this realization alone is not enough to make pragmatic changes. For any sort of positive change to take root mentally, you'll have to train your mind to be habituated to what is healthy and functional. This is especially important during times of discomfort and hardship. Instructing your mind in this way will take time and patience. If you train consistently, you'll experience remarkable benefits.

## Train the Mind, Transform the Brain

For decades neuroscientists claimed that the human brain was hard-wired in a particular way; they argued it couldn't change once fully formed. It is to our benefit that the idea of the unchanging human brain has been turned on its head—literally! As neuroscientists probe into the brain's neuroplasticity, or ability to change, they realize just how capable it truly is of being reshaped. A growing body of research analyzes how various messages and mental activities alter the brain's function and structure. Skills learned, decisions made, and actions taken all change the brain. The primary point of interest here is that your brain can change based solely on the thoughts you are thinking. Directing your mind can sculpt your brain and rewire it in ways that are helpful to you and the direction in which you want to lead your life.

Did you know that you transform your brain for the better when you train your mind? Since both the source of cognitive problems and the solution lie within you, it is your responsibility to rewire your brain. Neuroscientist Alvaro Pascual-Leone's experiment at Harvard Medical School backs up the brain's ability to reshape itself. He asked study participants to play the piano for five days so that he could measure their motor cortex using transcranial magnetic stimulation (TMS) tests. He discovered that each participant's repetitive finger movements impacted the physical structure of the surrounding areas of the motor cortex portion of their brain. Then he had another group of volunteers do the same piano practice, but only in their minds. He measured their motor cortex in the same way as the first group. After analyzing the two groups of participants, the group that practiced the piano mentally generated the same motor cortex results as the ones who did the exercises physically. This shows that through directing your mind repetitively, you can change the very structure of your brain.

One of the world's leading science journalists, Sharon Begley, wrote on the mind's ability to transform the brain. In her book *Train Your Mind, Change Your Brain,* Begley explores the powerful influence your mind has on upgrading your brain through mind training practices such as Buddhist mindfulness techniques. Through studies performed on people who practice mind training and cutting-edge techniques, neuroscientists can now examine the influence directing the energy of the mind has on the brain's physical structure. Currently, there is sizable proof that our brains undergo favorable modification through mind training practice. Neurological experimentation has been, and is still being, conducted on Buddhist monastics who have been practicing mind training for many years. Researchers measure using techniques such as TMS mapping, electroencephalography, computed tomography, and MRI scans to collect data. Begley identifies the pioneers in these scientific investigations, such as neuroscientist Richard Davidson of the University of Wisconsin–Madison. Davidson examined Buddhist monks' brain activity in the left prefrontal cortex, the area of the brain associated with contentment and happiness. As the monks meditated on compassion, he used an MRI to see what was going on in their brains. Not only did the more experienced compassion meditators display a greater link between the emotion and thinking centers in the brain, but the activity in their left prefrontal worked with the right prefrontal (associated with negative moods) in ways never seen before. This suggests, says Davidson, that happiness is a mental skill that you can develop through training your mind.

More extensive examinations have reconfirmed that areas of the brain associated with happiness are far more developed and active in those meditators who not only train their minds, but do so with an intention toward their hearts. This sort of training—training in wisdom and compassion—profoundly challenges one's self-absorption, taps into our interconnection, and encourages the mental activity responsible for generating a warm heart. We all want happiness, so that is worth more than money in the bank! Although they are not rich in the creature comforts and luxuries that the modern world offers, these humble meditators are billionaires in joy. They have harnessed the power of their minds and influenced their brains in the best and most positive way.

It is amazing how much mind training improves your brain. It opens new neural pathways associated with happiness. With ongoing practice, scientists are learning that you can dramatically influence your neuroplasticity for the better—you can rewire your thinking, generate new neurons, and change both the structure and size of your brain. Contemplative practices encourage your inner growth, brain health, and personal improvements. Furthermore, there is no age limit. The brain can adapt whether one is nine or ninety. If over the years you've experienced deep, scarring hardships, the mind training practices in this book can reshape your brain. They can help you rebound and better cope with trauma, illness, and any sort of disorders. This perspective means you are no longer a servant to your past, or even your genetic code, for a happy life. You can develop power over your thoughts and emotions rather than letting emotions and thoughts have power over you. When you train the energy of your mind, you fortify your innate superpowers.

## THE POWER OF THE MIND

One tremendous power I've witnessed the mind to have is the power to predict the future. In my thirties, while teaching at Sera Jey Monastic University, I volunteered to participate in a scientific experiment headed by a team of American and British researchers. These professional analysts sought out Buddhist monks who were adept at mind training. For their investigation, they asked me to practice my tradition's form of meditation for fifteen minutes. Afterward, they'd show me four pictures on a computer screen. But before showing me the pictures, I had to try to predict what the images would be. Once I made my guess, the computer would randomly select one of the pictures. Because the process was completely random, no one knew which picture would be chosen by the computer. We had to predict which picture it would be before the computer chose.

Initially, I considered the whole experiment a game; it didn't seem very serious. But then I saw how the researchers had divided participants into two groups. One group was made up of people who hadn't meditated, and the other group consisted of people who were experienced meditators. Later, I discovered that the experienced meditators could guess correctly which picture the computer would select far more often than those who had little experience meditating. I was curious to know what type of meditation garnered best results, so I seized the opportunity to do a little scientific inquiry on my own. I asked the participants what kind of meditation they did. I discovered that those who practiced compassion meditation had a greater prediction rate than those who didn't. In my Buddhist tradition, compassion is an essential spiritual practice. Consequently, I wasn't surprised that the selfless, compassionate meditation resulted in a more powerful outcome.

At the end of the experiment, a group of partnered psychologists visited. We asked them, "Have you discovered that the mind can know the future?" The team of psychologists replied that the mind definitely has the power to predict the future. This experiment was done in many different places, so they were looking for something that all people's minds have the potential for. My experience has taught me that the mind is similar to time, as both are a continuum from the past to the future. Therefore, it seems possible for the mind to travel ahead in time to perceive future events. This leads me to believe that the mind is mobile. In the Tibetan Buddhist tradition, we learn that the mind is divided into two parts: gross and subtle. Your gross mind depends on your body. When your body dies, we believe that your gross mind goes with it. The task of the gross mind is to send information it gets from the five senses to your subtle mind. We also believe that the subtle mind doesn't have a sense of "I" and moves from lifetime to lifetime. It's where your personal, karmic information is stored; some people might call it a soul. Your whole mind is in an interdependent relationship with your body, because your body is the container in which your mind functions. It is possible to access your subtle mind through contemplative meditation practices. I learned that wherever the subtle mind goes, it is accompanied by a faint wind energy. This faint wind energy forms the bridge connecting your body and your mind. Perhaps it's through this wind channel that your mind can heal your body.

## MIND AND BODY

Your mind influences your body and, consequently, your health. For example, a study performed by Bishop University's Erin Shackell and Lionel Standing examined whether mental training alone could produce muscle strength. They discovered that the participants who trained in their mind increased their physical strength by twenty-four percent, those who trained physically gained twenty-eight percent muscle strength, and the control group saw no changes. This is an essential principle in practice: mind over matter, so to speak. Yet what happens to your body if your mind is pessimistic? Since life is full of challenges, it can be overwhelming and result in a negative mental state. An excessive amount of this negative energy harms the physical health of your body. That is one reason why you must train your mind to generate positive mental states, which can counteract pessimism. Whenever possible, use your mind training practice to reduce negative energy. It will encourage better health.

Your mind can influence your body in the best way. Your mind has the power to help heal your body. I am not advising you to stop taking your medication and rely solely on mind training—that would be foolish. Rather, I hope to encourage your practice with the knowledge that there is a growing body of hopeful evidence that has found that the mind has the power to assist in healing the body and preventing disease. Researchers at Stanford Medicine—Stanford University's medical school and hospital system—urge medical communities to consider the importance of each patient's mindset and its relationship to healing. More than thirty years of neurobiological research at Stanford's research centers indicates that the placebo effect engages brain areas that can result in recovery. In other words, a treatment option that seems to be real but isn't, like a sugar pill, has been found to be just as effective as real treatments in some situations. This research verifies that a person's mindset and expectations impact whether a treatment will work.

Suppose you have the mindset that stress is a valuable part of life. According to research conducted by Stanford assistant professor Alia Crum, this type of rosy mental disposition toward stress results in greater well-being. Considering stress in this optimistic way leads to good health, emotional well-being, and work productivity. Kelly McGonigal, a health psychologist at Stanford and program developer for the Center for Compassion and Altruism Research and Education (CCARE), has made it a mission to understand the benefits of stress. She offers some simple stress advice. She suggests embracing the mindset that stress provides an opportunity to learn and grow. It is a natural biological response, and it helps create stress inoculation as your brain rewires and learns to handle stressors better. Learning to appreciate stress is valuable. Knowing that stress is helpful, that you can handle it, and that all people must face it, benefits you. Much like the placebo effect, your positive mindset alone can produce healthy results. On the flip side, research also concludes that a negative mindset can trigger unwanted adverse nocebo effects. This occurs for example when patients experience more pain after being told a shot will hurt or experience a side effect of medication after being made aware of it. The placebo effect and the nocebo effect demonstrate the clear connection between the type of thoughts in your mind and their effect on your well-being.

The placebo effect takes an exciting turn in Jo Marchant's book, *Cure: A Journey into the Science of Mind Over Body*. Marchant holds a PhD in genetics and microbiology, and she offers research on how our minds are influenced by another person's frame of mind. In one of her experiments, three groups of two hundred and sixty-two patients with irritable bowel syndrome were offered three different treatment experiences. The first group did not receive treatment. Group number two knowingly received a placebo from a cold, uncaring medical practitioner. The last group of test subjects knowingly received a placebo from a warm, caring medical practitioner. Of the three, which do you think had the best results? Perhaps without surprise, it was the last group. This points out that your mindset can influence not only yourself but those around you.

## MIND AND WATER

Can your mindset affect water? Some people, such as Japanese researcher Masaro Emoto, believe that it can. He claims that adopting a specific mental state while expressing emotionally charged words toward water affects its frozen crystal formation. This can even happen at a distance. In the *Journal for Scientific Exploration,* a triple-blind replication of how distant intention affects water crystals was performed by the Institute of Noetic Sciences. Nineteen hundred people from Austria and Germany were asked to do a prayer of gratitude directed toward water containers at a specific laboratory in California. The water containers that received the positive intentions were held inside an electromagnetically shielded room thousands of miles away. The water was later frozen and then examined by 2,500 non-biased participants. The participants didn't know the underlying treatment conditions. Other water containers acted as proximal and distant controls. What was discovered was that the water that received the prayers of gratitude developed more aesthetically pleasing crystals then those that did not receive the good intentions. Curious to see just how much influence a person's mind has on water, I asked one of my inquisitive lay students to perform a similar experiment. He used several separate water containers. One container he chanted a mantra next to daily for forty days, and the others he didn't. Day after day, photos were taken to record how the water containers had changed. The water he chanted over remained clear, whereas the other water had begun to get murky and change color.

I decided to carry out a similar experiment with one of my young students. We got two cups of water, and I told him to adopt an angry mindset and shout at one cup of water and do the opposite to another cup of water. The student was only nine years old, so his attention span was still short. He only did the experiment for two or three days before getting bored and throwing both cups of water away! We will never know the outcome of that experiment. This goes to show that we need to be able to focus our attention in the first place to experience any results. But I am left wondering. Since we're made mostly of water, does our mindset, and the energy of the words we choose, affect us and those around us?

## TRANSFORMING YOUR REALITY

Scientific studies confirm that words affect us and those around us deeply. There is an energy and a meaning behind words, which is why it is a mistake to think that they do not have some power. When you choose your words mindfully, whether those words are an inner dialogue or outer dialogue, you have the power to affect yourself and others for the better. Positive words can strengthen the brain's prefrontal lobe and make you more resilient to physical and emotional stress. The book *Words Can Change Your Brain*, written jointly by neuroscientist Andrew Newberg and communication expert Mark Waldman, confirms the power of words. These two experts offer proof that merely one word can influence the expression of genes that regulate emotional and physical stress. They also confirm that thoughts can change how you perceive your reality. Holding one positive view in your mind can benefit your brain and motivate you. That is why I often encourage my students to keep one simple affirmation in their minds, which is: "Live strong and happily!" That is also why I advocate mind training. Focused, contemplative, analytical mind training uses the power of your mind to master your inner dialogue; it encourages you to think positive, wholesome thoughts, which in turn generate happiness.

Some mind-training practitioners can be happy even in the most uncomfortable, stressful circumstances. A while back, I visited a fellow practitioner who was sixty years old. He was in the last stages of a deadly disease, and there was no cure for his illness. When I met with him, I was sure that he'd be irritable. He was seriously unwell, so he hadn't been able to eat for quite some time. Unexpectedly, he wasn't irritable. Instead of being upset, he felt gratitude. "I am so grateful and happy to have lived until sixty. Many people die before this age. I'm just pleased I have lived this long," he said. My colleague was able to see the positive side despite suffering from a major illness as well as experiencing the discomforts of hunger and being near death. When your mind is trained, you have the power to rise above problems and see that there are many things to be appreciative of in your life. When you train your mind, you open yourself up to a well of gratitude and feel the joy that comes with it.

As you learn how your choices affect your life, the question is, will you choose to practice mind training or not? If you do, not only will you gain the superpowers mentioned, but you'll also develop the power of good decision-making. According to the science of neuroplasticity, your mind can shape part of your central processing center, positively influencing the choices that affect your life. Additional research published by the School of Psychology and School of Economics, South China Normal University, in the journal *Frontiers in Psychology* infers that training your mind regulates brain activities associated with emotion regulation, empathy, and cognitive control. It leads to improvements in ethical decision-making, both socially and for oneself. That means that mind training is also ethics training. This training inspires you to *not* engage in things like lying, stealing, hurting, or using cruel words. All the more if your training includes not just your mind but your heart. Meditation helps you be more intuitive, which in turn makes making healthy, honest, and wise choices much easier.

This reminds me of a story about a practitioner who developed her intuition. There was once a young woman who was eager to have a lovely wedding, so she decided to get married. It was an incredible ceremony; however, just three months later, there was another kind of legal custom: a divorce! Depressed and lamenting her poor decision, she decided her best option was to seek out a teacher of mind training. After several months of mind training, one day she was told to do walking meditation. As she mindfully shuffled down the walkway, directing her attention to the movement of her feet, she heard a small inner voice whisper, "Don't take one more step." The woman listened, immediately stopped, and a great boulder fell just before her. She stood dumbfounded at the voice's accuracy. She asked, "Who are you?" Her inner voice softly replied, "I am your intuition." She crossly replied, "Where were you when I was getting married?" Clearly, she developed the "superpower" of discernment during the time that she had engaged in mind training practices. If only she had started training to build her superpowers sooner. But, like most of us, obstacles got in the way.

## PATIENCE AND TIME

Once you overcome obstacles, you will gain superpowers. When you train your mind, you'll grow more powerful with each practice. Trust your place in this vast interconnected universe. If you have your doubts, remember you are part of a magnificent whole and play an important part in it. To use the computer analogy, if you take a piece of hardware out, it will not function. And because you are part of a whole, consequently, any improvements you make for yourself will help improve everything around you. This is the truth, and you need to have faith in this truth of the dependency of all things. So please, when you find an obstacle, stay the course, use your practice, and work through it.

In his book *War and Peace*, Leo Tolstoy wrote, "Patience is waiting. Not passively waiting. That is laziness. But to keep going when the going is hard and slow—that is patience. The two most powerful warriors are patience and time." These are useful words. Be patient with your progress and limitations but don't give up. Be patient like you would with a child or a puppy or kitten that you must potty train. You certainly wouldn't harm your kitten if it piddled outside of the box, would you? Give the process time. Sometimes we don't think we have the time. In our pursuit of happiness, many of us suffer from too-busy-itis! In reality, we can spare a little time. Practice can be done almost anywhere, and the best practice is practice done in daily life. You are not nearly as busy as you think. Work and studies may be time-consuming, but sometimes we become confused between busyness and personal value. Although type-A workaholic behavior has been glorified and considered a status marker, it isn't what is best for you. In Italy, for example, being too busy is considered very humdrum. Maybe that is why Rome wasn't built in a day? Nevertheless, this is how a lot of people live their lives.

Many of us live moving between school, work, marriage, and family. We jump from surfing the internet to gaming, then streaming videos and checking our social media feeds. Our minds are consumed with one thing after another in constant pursuit of joy and serenity. I ask you to consider what sort of life you really want for yourself. Do you want a life where you jump from thing to thing while you wait for your annual vacations or a life with solid, consistent joy, regardless of your circumstances? It would be a much better use of your precious time to train your mind and apply what you learn from your practice. Then you can enjoy life regardless of whether you are on holiday or in traffic. You can delight in existence no matter where you are. That includes when you are at places like work or school, since that is how many of us spend the bulk of our waking lives.

You've read all these studies, stories, and examples, but what is the point? To sum it up, you have control over your life, because that control is all based on your mind. Each year, scientists have grown increasingly supportive of what we Buddhist monks have known about the mind all along. They have learned that the mind can be harnessed and used to benefit not only yourself but everything that is part of this infinite network of energy. It would be best if you overcame your limited notion of self and others to do this. You must also begin to understand the importance of taming your mind and using your heart. You'll have to value what your heart offers, which you can accomplish through mind training practices. Be realistic, though; slow progress is better than no progress. Take responsibility for your mind's health and your life's direction. Gradually, through regular mind training practice, you'll build a nest for your thoughts to rest. That way, if you have a fear flying around your mind like me, you can practice! Before long, that fear will fly away.

# Reflection

On a particularly windy day, a wise teacher said to his students, "Look at those tree branches swaying back and forth in the wind. Which is moving: the wind, the tree branches, or perhaps something else?"

"It's the wind, of course! The wind is causing the branches to move," exclaimed one enthusiastic student. "No, it's the branches that are moving, obviously! You can't see the wind move," argued another student.

After listening to much debate and the various replies offered by his students, the teacher responded, "It's neither the wind moving nor the tree branches. What's actually moving is nothing other than your own mind."

Your mind is naturally fickle; it frequently changes based on many factors, such as your interests or emotions. Thoughts take flight at the slightest provocation. Refrain from being surprised or overly concerned when you notice your mind doesn't want to settle on a particular object, especially at first. It will be best if you increase your attention span slowly.

When it comes to a human's ability to focus, did you know that . . . oh look, a goldfish! Have you heard that goldfish have an average attention span of nine seconds? Some days you may feel like a goldfish yourself, your attention bouncing from place to place. I, however, have discovered our potential for developing attention to be quite contrary to this goldfish brain. From my experience, it is possible to remain focused on the same object for a very long time, but it takes practice. You can train your mind to be highly concentrated. There's no reason to worry if you find that, at first, you cannot keep your attention on the point of focus. Keep gently bringing your mind back to the focal point whenever you notice it's wandered off. Practice like that every day!

You can practice whenever you have a few minutes to spare. It is okay to practice this kind of meditation anywhere; you needn't be in solitude at home, sitting cross-legged with your eyes closed. Mindfulness meditation—where you repeatedly bring your mind back to focusing on one thing to stabilize the mind, induce steady awareness, and strengthen focus—is simply an activity done with your mind, so you need not solely sit. The most important thing is to develop mental concentration. You can practice while walking, working, cooking, or lying down. Although lying down is not the best posture, sometimes your time is limited and it's all the time you can spare. If that is so, practicing focusing on your breath while lying in bed at night might be your best option. You still must keep keenly focused, even though you're in a reclining posture, and try not to fall asleep. If your mind is too distracted, another possibility is to use the sound of your inner voice, or outer voice if you must, as a focal point. Slowly and repeatedly count from one to twenty-five, then repeat. Do this for five or ten minutes. As you advance, you can visualize an object, like an apple, and focus on that. Throughout your day, try to practice using what you are doing as a focal point for your attention for as long as you are comfortably able to. If you can focus more than nine seconds, you may have out-focused a goldfish!

# CHAPTER 9

# Caring and Sharing

PROPER MIND TRAINING includes heart training. The Dalai Lama said, "If you want others to be happy, practice compassion. If you want to be happy, practice compassion." The society in which you live may have you believing that a better place to live and a more luxurious car is what it takes to live a joyful life. Or perhaps you're brainwashed into thinking that the latest clothing styles, advanced technologies, delicious food, or a higher salary will make you happy. The social norms around you can condition you into believing that the more you consume, the happier you will be. That is what makes sales events like Black Friday so dangerous. But it doesn't matter how much you consume; you can't fill an empty feeling inside of you with things. You can experience some fleeting satisfaction eating an ice cream cone on a hot day, though if you're lactose intolerant, it's even more fleeting. This type of pleasure is not what you are after. You can't find lasting joy in the material world. According to a study by Jessica Cerretani in *Harvard Medicine* on the science of emotions, happiness is related to numerous factors. Some of these we can't easily control, like evolution. For example, a person's predisposition to pessimism is in part due to their drive to survive. But there are other factors that are in your control. Since researching sadness is more lucrative then studying happiness, there is less data on the subject, but researchers have discovered that joy is in part derived from healthy relationships. The warm emotional disposition of a caring mother or a friend can transform your sorrow into joy.

Emotions are contagious. Nicholas Christakis, Harvard Medical School professor of medical sociology and medicine, researched the contagion of emotions within social networks. His research suggests that emotions do spread through communities. For those who train their mind, this is great to hear! Mind training strengthens your ability to be a positive contagion. It trains your mind to be rid of self-fixation and of things like self-pity, and helps you consider others outside of you. For real satisfaction in life, it is necessary to pay attention to others. There is a deep connection between your own joy and the mental and emotional disposition found in the world around you. If just one person in your family is discontented, there is a risk that you may catch their dissatisfaction. But if one person is happy . . . well, you know. Mental and emotional dispositions within social groups are infectious, which is why you need to live strong. You need to be able to guard your mind from negative influences. One of the best ways to do this is to build compassion. You train your mind to deeply comprehend that you're not the only one prone to suffering. No one is exempt from encountering difficulties.

## TRAINING FOR HANDLING THE INEVITABLE

There is a story about a grief-stricken mom who experienced hardship and a tremendous despair when she lost her young child to illness. She loved her child immensely, so the loss hit her extremely hard. In an act of ruthless desperation, she sought someone she believed could bring her child back to life. "Please!" she implored them. "My child has only recently passed. Can you revive her?" Sensing her maddening grief at the loss of her beloved child, they responded in kind. "Yes, I will bring your dear, departed child back to life if you can bring me a mustard seed from someone who hasn't encountered death." Filled with wishful thinking, the woman immediately searched far and wide, but to no avail. Regardless of the variety of different people she encountered, everyone she spoke with had experienced the loss of someone they cared for. After a long and exhausting search, she finally realized that no such mustard seed existed. It was then that she fully comprehended that everyone faces similar difficulties.

The news is a constant reminder that all people face difficulties, but did you know that watching those tragedies can cause you pain? According to a study in the *International Journal of Behavior Medicine*, the news is bad news for you. Researchers Attila Szabo and Katey L. Hopkinson discovered that watching the news triggers persistent, negative feelings that could only be transformed through directed psychological intervention. Two groups of people were asked to watch fifteen minutes of a random newscast. Afterward, all the participants experienced state anxiety and total mood disturbance, or TMD, as well as a decrease in positive affect. One group was relieved of these negative consequences by engaging in a progressive relaxation exercise. The control group, however, attended a lecture afterward, which gave them no relief. Since tragedies dominate the headlines and emotions are contagious, it stands to reason that negativity rubs off on the watcher.

If widespread coverage of others' tragedies has such a strong effect on us, why do we still perceive ourselves as separate from others? Even if you don't watch the news, surely you encounter someone like a sick work colleague, whose suffering gives you a sense of discomfort. How can you deny the mental and emotional connection you have with them? If you deeply understand your oneness, do you also consider your effect on the world? Mind training will help you answer these questions. A big part of training your mind is strengthening the insight necessary to handle the inevitable mental and emotional troubles that are part of ordinary life. When you do this type of mind training, you develop both wisdom *and* compassion; one alone won't do, because both are needed for the cultivation of emotional intelligence. In my tradition of Buddhism, when you train your mind toward the wisdom of the truth, you train it toward your heart. You use wise, focused, analytical, and contemplative practices to engage healthily with the world. Regular mind training practice like this helps you endure, and then transform, issues in your everyday life into joy.

## THE UNEXPECTED PRESENT

I recall an incident while traveling that describes what happens once your mind is trained to care for others. Once, I was at the airport in Nepal to catch a flight back to Tibet. Like everyone else, I had to go through a security check. To my surprise, one of the guards found a very nice Swiss army knife in my luggage. He told me that I could take the Swiss army knife with me, but I would have to go back to the baggage check-in area, fill out a form, and go back to some other place. The process was so long and complicated. Since I didn't know how I got the knife in the first place, I thought the guard might appreciate such a gift, so I gave it to him. He beamed at receiving such an unexpected and useful present.

After the flight, when I got to my destination, I called my mom. She excitedly asked if I had seen the gift that she had snuck into one of the pockets of my luggage. I then deduced she was talking about the Swiss army knife. Even though I was feeling remorse for giving away her gift, I expressed my appreciation to her and then asked her how much she spent on such a thoughtful present. She said it was fifty Swiss francs, several thousand Nepalese rupees! This was a lot of money for my mom. For the first few minutes of our call, I felt so much regret for giving away such a lovely, thoughtful, and pricey gift. Then my trained mind quickly started to think about the positive aspects of giving the knife away. I thought about how the guard radiated happiness after receiving such an excellent present. Then I thought about how he'd tell his family and friends about how he received something so unpredictable from a monk. I imagined how they'd feel so happy for him. I really felt glad for that guard. The more I reflected like this, the better I felt. Even today, when I look back on this experience, it gives me a good feeling. You see, when your mind turns toward your heart, you generate goodwill and, in turn, feel joy.

## EMPATHETIC UNDERSTANDING

A big part of mind training is accepting the cold, hard fact that everyone alive encounters troubles and loss. I may have lost my Swiss army knife, but I didn't lose my heart. The biggest loss of all is losing your caring heart. You may lose your kindness and compassion if you don't consider that the suffering you are feeling is the same suffering that everyone else endures. Remind yourself that by knowing your own suffering, you know others' suffering. This is especially tricky when you've found yourself in hard times. Because if you have yet to develop a strong, compassionate mind, you lack the inner tools to cope with your suffering and may resort to things like self-pity and blame. Feeling like a victim of challenging times leads to a lousy case of GAS, which can blind you to the pain of others. That's why it's vital to deeply comprehend that your happiness is dependent on understanding that you and everyone around you are riding these stormy seas together on the same boat. Misfortune can make you GASSY, but when you grow in insight, and the truth it provides, you grow in empathetic understanding.

Training your mind means training your heart. Developing deep awareness of the precious knowledge that we are in this together generates your love, kindness, and compassion for all. Creating your habitual consideration of this truth of oneness gives rise to the courage to face life's difficulties. It builds your confidence and incites you to take meaningful action to be a positive influence on others. After all, when I say compassion, I'm not talking about just feeling someone's pain, although that is part of it. It isn't just empathy. It is seeing past the facade and truly recognizing that we all suffer. Compassion is the willful act of caring and sharing. It is the heartfelt choice to treat someone with sensitivity and be to someone what they need most, based on their circumstance.

During the height of the COVID-19 pandemic, people were singing from their balconies to raise the spirits of others in quarantine—this is but one powerful demonstration of our inclination to care. That crowds of people were cheering on their exhausted healthcare workers is a testament to our innate compassion. If you find it difficult to see the value of such acts, you may have lost sight of your caring heart. Without empathetic understanding, your mind can become unsteady and hypersensitive. You may not fully comprehend your authentic connection to others and instead feel like you face challenging times alone. Thinking of just yourself causes mental instability, such that one small change in the environment results in you feeling emotionally distraught; then another small change comes along, and you're happy again. This kind of instability or state of constant change is what's meant by "emotional roller coaster." The mind and the heart are close—much like the self and others. Your mind impacts your heart, and vice versa.

When you lack love and compassion in your life, you experience immense mental difficulty and painful suffering. There is quite a bulk of psychological and medical studies on the lasting impact of child and infant neglect. Despite having their basic needs met, babies that suffer from a lack of affection have a higher mortality rate. Babies that do survive neglect suffer throughout their life from things like social withdrawal, poor impulse control, problems regulating emotions, difficulty coping, poor self-esteem, tantrums, self-punishment, and low academic achievement. From this long list, we can see how powerful caring and sharing can be. With this chapter's practice, you can begin to think about the suffering of those around you, whether your family, community, friends, or anyone else. If you do this regularly, you'll start to cultivate compassion and, eventually, the feeling of love. Many people understand these connections, but don't know how to put compassion into practice. This practice also asks you to release any misconceptions that meditation, or mind training, is just sitting quietly for your own benefit only.

## COMPASSION NEEDS WISDOM

This reminds me of someone whose meditation on compassion got the attention of the locals. In a small country village, word spread of a visiting meditator who was passionate about his focus on compassion. For days the meditator sat cross-legged with his eyes closed in the village square until one day, a curious bystander asked him a question. "Since you've spent all this time focused on compassion, I wonder, if you had two iPads, would you give one to someone in need?" The meditator replied, "Oh yes, of course." Again, the villager asked, "If you had two computers, would you also give one of them away?" Similarly, the meditator responded, "Yes, without a doubt!" Still curious, the bystander asked, "And if you had two smartphones, would you do the same with one of them?" The meditator immediately responded, "Two smartphones? No, I would not give one of them away." Surprised at the meditator's sudden lack of charity, the villager asked, "You said that you would readily give away one of your iPads and one of your computers. They are normally far more expensive! So why wouldn't you give your smartphone to the needy?" The meditator replied, "Well, this is because I don't actually have iPads or computers. But I do have a couple of smartphones." Obviously, there are levels of achievement when it comes to practicing compassion. This meditator apparently had so far only focused on compassion in theory, rather than practice—but we must start somewhere. First, we must start our practice at the most basic level, the level of mind.

In the beginning, training in compassion is done purely on the mental level. Mind training becomes actuality when you use your heart to give to the needy. But if you reach this high level, it is imperative to utilize your analytical reasoning and critical thinking skills to assess whether your generosity is skillful or not. There is a considerable danger in engaging in heart-centered practices without using the fullness of your intellect. It's important for you to take into consideration the reality of the situation. When it comes to matters of the heart, you mustn't fully trust in someone, or something, without first applying analysis. I discovered the danger of having compassion without using wisdom when I was a teacher at Sera Jey University.

Once a beggar came to the monastery saying that his mother was in the hospital and that he needed financial help for her treatment. I felt a lot of compassion for him, but it was untested. Without getting details, I simply gave him three hundred rupees and told him that I would help him more later. I encouraged him to promptly take his mom to the hospital and told him to bring all her bills to me, so I could provide continual financial support. He gave me his name and his address and then left. About an hour or two later a nagging doubt crept into my mind. I told someone to go and check to see if the information he gave me was legit or not. Another hour later, I got a telephone call confirming that I'd been tricked, that the name and address the man gave me didn't exist. He also said this man was a well-known con artist.

At that time, I wondered, "How was I so easily fooled?" That's why you must always investigate all things very carefully. Even though I got conned, I thought, "This man is truly a benefit to me because I learned something fundamental." I genuinely learned a lot from this experience, which had eluded me throughout years of studying the teachings on the importance of wisdom and compassion. I discovered that true discernment is the result of not only using your kind heart, but also using your wise mind. If you solely let your heart guide you, you won't make intelligent, well-rounded, healthy choices. That is why real-life experience is so precious. It allows us to take a step beyond mental practice. I am very appreciative of that con artist. Several months later, I bumped into him somewhere. I told him how he had really taught me so much and thanked him for the lesson. As you see, using your intelligence is very important in practicing compassion.

Compassion relies on some mental analysis. That is why analytical and contemplative mind training includes heart training. You need an intelligent heart! If you have some doubt regarding the honesty of the person in front of you, it is all right not to be charitable. Whether you give money or do not give money really has nothing to do with your practice. Rather, being appropriately helpful will become second nature to you once you have reached a higher level of practice. You can then do away with all this mental analysis. You will instinctually give whatever is necessary without a second thought. Mind you, this is a very high level of attainment. And I want to warn you: before you reach the stage of incorporating wisdom with compassion, there is the real danger of feeling regret, as I did when I gave money to the con artist. You might think, "Oh, I've been duped! I should not have been so foolishly generous!" This might lead you to ditch your practice. At this early stage, it is more important to generate compassion within your mind without engaging in outward actions. Otherwise, conflict and misunderstanding may arise, which can easily interfere with any understanding you have generated mentally.

My father struggles in this way. He used to quarrel frequently with my mom. Since he has adopted the practice of compassion, instead of getting defensive, shutting down, or retorting, he now tries to pay attention to what she says so he can understand her point of view. He gives her the chance to speak. As a result, disputes between them end quickly. Compassion begins with taking the time and effort to understand others. To truly listen. Begin with community members, your loved ones, and friends. You must train to be attentive of the world around you. Train your mind to consider, listen, and understand others.

## SHARING AND CARING

To truly care, you must try to understand where someone is coming from. Attentive listening and consideration are critical. I recall an incident when I was a teacher at the monastic institute where one of my teenage students suddenly became uncharacteristically distant and very lax in his studies. He stopped paying attention in the classroom and eventually began skipping class entirely. When I asked him what was going on, he remained sullen and quiet. Initially, I chalked it up to teenage angst and neglected to find out what was really troubling him. I merely scolded him about his bad attitude and his poor schoolwork performance. That caused him to become even more distant, which concerned me, so I began to ask around. About a week later, I discovered from a colleague that the reason why he was so glum was because he was concerned for his mom's safety. The teen confessed to being haunted by witnessing his father brutally beat his mother on a recent visit home. The abuse was so severe that his mom had suffered kidney damage.

I realized that his recollection of his mom being hurt, and his concern for her well-being, prevented him from concentrating on anything, let alone his schoolwork. After hearing of his situation, I reapproached him with compassion. I pulled him aside and gently asked him if he was worried about his mom's safety. Sensing my genuine concern, he burst into tears. From that point forward, he shared with me his painful emotions, which in turn emboldened my heart to care. I learned a lot from that interaction of sharing and caring. It helped me further grasp the importance of compassionate understanding. Compassion is not only helpful for those who are suffering; it also offers you the precious opportunity to mature emotionally and strengthen your heart. Helping others helps you.

## KINDNESS AND COMPASSION

Compassion always touches on the deepest truth of our interconnection. It elevates our human spirit. There have been historic feats of compassion even in times of great strife. Victor Frankl's book, *Man's Search for Meaning*, emphasizes the value of care and kindness amid the horrific suffering within Nazi Germany's concentration camps. He wrote that those who survived the concentration camp remember the few compassionate individuals who chose to comfort others. They remembered the ones who gave away their last morsel of bread despite facing starvation themselves. The self-sacrifice that these warm-hearted individuals had shown are confirmation that compassion is an everlasting choice. It sticks in the heart of humankind and reverberates through time. Frankl wrote, "Everything can be taken from a man but one thing: the last of the human freedoms—to choose one's attitude in any given set of circumstances, to choose one's own way." Frankl, who was himself a concentration camp survivor, was witness to humankind's heroic nature. He saw our ability to rise above apathy, make wise choices, suppress irritability, and preserve freedom of choice even while under acute stress. Therefore, despite dire circumstances, we are given an option to rise out of our own personal difficulties in order to sincerely care for our fellow human beings. If others who are directly facing their mortality can generate this level of kindness and compassion, then certainly you can!

We often think that compassion is something we ought to feel for disaster victims on the other side of the world. In fact, it's often the case that the people most in need of our tenderness are right in front of us: our family, friends, coworkers, and community. Properly caring for another person begins with listening, in order to understand their problems and point of view. Understanding is easy to do when you are in the same situation, but we all have so many different points of view and circumstances. It is a real challenge to genuinely empathize with another. Furthermore, it is particularly hard to comprehend others if your state of mind is diametrically opposed to the one you are attempting to understand. Still, compassion always begins with grasping the depth of someone's suffering. Start with those closest.

Not too long ago, there was a gasoline shortage where I live. My brother and I needed fuel, so we went to the gas station, where we had to wait in line for four hours. When we finally got to the pump, the attendants only gave us about four gallons of gasoline. Once we had our gas, I looked back at all the other people who were still waiting and said to one of them, "It must be hard to wait for such a long time for such a small amount of gas." The person replied, "Oh no, it is much better now! In the past, we had to wait for ten hours!" This shows you how despite being in a similar situation, people will have differing points of view and sometimes contradictory outlooks. Differing perspectives are typical, so strive to empathetically comprehend others.

Because so many of us tend to be self-centered and protective of our ego, listening to what someone else is saying is often not easy. Especially when someone criticizes you. You instinctively react with aversion and defensiveness. But your refusal to listen makes matters even more difficult. It's not just a matter of listening to what people say; you also have to be willing to acknowledge you've understood what they convey, even if it's critical of you. The more you advance in your practice of turning your mind toward compassionate understanding, the more your inner strength builds, and the more you're able to extend your heart to those you find displeasing. You don't just care, but you share their burden. I don't mean sharing your unsolicited advice—you share you time and attention, and take on their troubles. When they are upset, you try to understand more deeply by going to the dark place with them. Once you share an understanding, compassion compels you to want to alleviate their suffering. Then when the time is right, the two of you can share a smile.

## ONE WITH THE WORLD

You are in a relationship with the world around you. That means your happiness relies on the well-being of your environment. When those around you suffer, so do you. Yet universal compassion, meaning compassion that includes those we despise and dislike, is not an easy task! If it were easy, you'd show concern and care for drivers that ride your tail and honk at you, or for someone who just rudely flipped you off or robbed you. At first, training your mind to develop the ability to be compassionate may be arduous. That is part of the reason that you must start with those closest to you. Begin with yourself, your family, your pets, and your community. The more you advance in your practice of turning your mind toward caring and sharing, the more your inner strength builds, and the more you're able to extend your heart to those you find displeasing.

While practicing, it is imperative to remain conscious of the connection between your mind and your heart. To train your mind properly, you must develop a heart that cares and shares. Once, I saw an article in the newspaper about a watch that runs on a person's kinetic energy. It made me wonder, what if our world ran on the energy of compassion? How much better would the world be? In my opinion, the world would be vastly better for all. That is why you must train your mind to value other beings. When you train your mind like this, you acknowledge and trust in your oneness with the world. Discovering this insight, you see that the world reflects not only your mind but also the warmth of your kind heart.

When you transform through generating a wise mind and a kind heart, you are happier. In turn, those in your immediate circle feel joy. Once the folks in your immediate circle are more joyful, your communities begin to reflect this happiness. Believe it or not, if you stay the course, the entire nation will soon follow—then the world. We all have the potential to stamp out suffering and encourage genuine joy, not just for ourselves, but for all. To do this you need to develop a meaningful way of life that nurtures growth through wisdom and compassion. You need a method to help you transform how you live. A tried-and-true way that promotes understanding, integrity, hope, unity, presence, kindness, and consistency. That method is detailed at the end of this book. No one is entitled to happiness, but without a doubt, through determination and mind training practice, you can turn your mind to wisdom and compassion. You can "live strong and happily!"

## Reflection

Every fall, a farmer would plow his field with his oxen in the foothills of the mountains. In the afternoon, he'd unyoke his strong beasts to give them time to graze and recharge. While he tilled the land by hand, his oxen went missing. The farmer looked all around his property, but he couldn't find his invaluable farmhands anywhere. Losing them made the farmer upset. He searched fervently, making his way deeper into the mountains. Angry, exhausted, and hungry, he decided to rest under a tree. Next to him, he found several *tinduka* fruits, which he scarfed down hungrily. Feeling starved, he set out to find the source. Close by, he saw a tinduka tree rooted in a cliffside by a waterfall that cascaded into a cavernous pit. He looked carefully and saw a big bunch of fruit hanging high in the tree. Feeling confident of his strength, he climbed his way to the top. As he climbed, several branches broke, sending him plummeting into the deep pool of water far below. Once he surfaced, he realized there was no way out. He was in a deep pit, so he wept tears of desperation. As night fell, he was attacked by a swarm of hungry mosquitos, only adding to his misery. The miserable farmer spent five days living on the pool water and a few squashed, rotten tindukas that had dropped from the tree high above.

On the sixth day, a beautiful ape visited the tinduka tree to pick some fruit. Seeing the sorry state of the gaunt farmer below, the ape felt compassion for the man. She would never like to be in such a situation. "It looks like you are in a jam, dear sir!" she exclaimed. "Yes, observant, strong ape. While looking for my oxen, I fell into this pit. I fear I will die of starvation if I don't get out soon!" Feeling immense pity for the man, she immediately started throwing fruit down for him to eat. "Don't worry!" she shouted. "There must be some way out!" After much consideration, she deduced that the only solution was to climb down the rocky cliff and give him a piggyback ride up. Once down, the man could see that he was much heavier than the small ape. Still, he climbed on her back, and she made her way slowly up the treacherous cliffside. It was a demanding and painful climb. Scaling the cliff exhausted the poor ape, but she didn't give up, and though it took half a day, they made it to the top. Completely worn out from the climb, she asked the man if he would kindly guard her against wild animals while she slept and recovered. "Yes, of course, I promise to protect you. Anything for my hero. Rest as long as you wish," he said.

As the ape lay fast asleep, the farmer got a wicked idea. "There is no way I'll make it out of the mountains eating just fruit. I will need to eat some meat to keep up my stamina." He looked at the ape as she lay deep in slumber, eyeing how much meat she had on her bones. "This ape's life doesn't matter as much as mine. I have a farm, and people rely on me." The farmer picked up a large rock to kill the caring ape, then threw it at her head. In his weakened state, he had no aim, so it grazed the ape's skull, causing her to bolt upright to confront her attacker. She looked around and saw only the farmer. At first, she was utterly speechless at the thought of him wanting to hurt her. Then, given that she was such a warm-hearted creature, her shock turned to profound sadness. "How could you do this? You promised to protect me after I saved you from sure death!" The man stood there, terrified that the ape would rip him apart for his wickedness. "You have saddened me, farmer. I may have taken you out of a hole, but your evil deed has put you into something far worse. Into a pit of cruelty!"

The farmer just stood there trembling, uncertain of his fate. "Come," she said. "I will take you to the edge of the mountain and show you the way to your village. But you must go first because I don't trust you." The speechless farmer felt overcome by the righteousness of the ape. After she had showed him the way back to the village, her parting words were, "Thank you for the lesson, farmer. I pity you even more now than when you were stuck in that pit. I know that what you do returns to you. My compassion will return to me, just as your selfish misdeed will return to you."

When you encounter someone in distress and feel their pain, compassion makes your heart quiver and urges you to want to eliminate or lessen their suffering. Even though your concern is a priceless human reaction, genuine compassion also originates in caring for yourself. Part of being responsible for yourself is acknowledging the importance of using both your head and your heart. Compassion without using your head can make you a big-hearted fool. Caring must include proper discernment, otherwise your undiscerning kindness can land you in big trouble, like the ape. Please always use your mind when operating your heart. Consider all the factors, including things like your own and others' selfish tendencies and GAS, interdependence, and causality. When you use wisdom to discern the right course of action, you may find it more compassionate to practice tough love. Have a smart heart! That way, you can determine what is *really* best.

When you look at a statue of Buddha, there is an aura around him. His halo is not just light, but represents the positive energy created by wise compassion. The energy of compassion is potent and benefits you and others mentally, physically, and spiritually. When compassion is paired with kindness, it strengthens your belief that you are a caring person. The force of a compassionate mind drives acts of kindness. Compassion is something that you experience inside of you; it has the quality of empathy, sympathy, and concern. You can direct compassion outward toward others or inward toward yourself; either way, it is a motivator to alleviate suffering. Kindness is a behavior that everyone can see and has the quality of friendliness, warmth, affection, and playfulness. What is remarkable about this is that when you develop and then act on love and compassion toward others, you will receive love and compassion in return. Though while it is essential to consider yourself in these scenarios too, don't let your selfishness blind you.

As you recall, many people are responsible for getting your toilet paper on store shelves. When you fail to recognize the significance of your dependency on this world, you fail to regard all beings as indispensable to your existence. You remain blind to the support others show you. This sort of ignorance of the truth leads to a judgmental attitude. You suffer by separating yourself from the world and making divisions between those who are right or wrong, friends or enemies, and so on. This divisive way of thinking discourages wise compassion and causes you to suffer from jealousy, GAS, negativity, and afflictive emotions.

An antidote to a lack of compassion is to contemplate suffering. It is not necessary to set aside time for this contemplative practice. Since it is an antidote to the problem of your cold-heartedness, this practice should be done the moment that you feel uncaring or the moment that you discover that your self-centered thinking is interfering with feelings of compassion. Start by reflecting on your own suffering. What is it that is causing your suffering? How does it feel? What would make you feel better? Let your reflection inspire a sense of understanding and care. Then thoroughly consider the suffering of someone close to you; someone like a family member, pet, or friend. Do they suffer with afflictions in a similar way? What do you think might alleviate their suffering? Once you grasp what someone close to you endures, move on to a neighbor, then a neutral person you have no strong feelings toward, then an enemy whom you do have strong feelings toward, then your whole community, and lastly the world. Consider those in the world who are worse off than you. For example, if you suffer with a particular disease, consider people who have the same disease, but do not have access to proper medical care or medicine. Gradually move your circle of empathetic understanding further and further outward until you include all beings. Reflection, in this way, sows lasting seeds of wise understanding and compassion inside of you. If practiced repeatedly, these seeds will grow and one day blossom into acts of true kindness.

# Preliminaries for an Effective Practice

O N A SUNNY autumn day, a large colony of ants were busily drying out the abundant grain they had stored over the summer. Seeing the enormous mounds of food shining in the sunlight, a hungry grasshopper offered to play a song on his fiddle for a bite to eat. "Why barter, musical grasshopper? Surely you have some stored food of your own," said the head ant. "Not yet, but there is plenty of time for such an arduous task. Instead, I thought it more important to take advantage of the warm summer weather by playing my fiddle and frolicking in a field of wildflowers. I'm sure I'll get around to gathering for my winter storage sooner or later," replied the grasshopper. "What?" The ant was shocked. "Winter is coming soon, and you haven't adequate food storage? I hate to tell you, grasshopper, but it's too late for you to gather food for the entire winter. What were you thinking?" The grasshopper wrung his hands in worry. The ant colony stopped what they were doing and looked at the grasshopper in pity. "Sorry grasshopper, we only have enough for our colony." With that said, the ants continued preparing their food to store for the winter, leaving the anxious grasshopper to his last-minute search for grain.

## DON'T PUT OFF MIND TRAINING

You cannot escape the responsibility of tomorrow by avoiding it today. I hope you are not like the grasshopper, putting off today for what you'll need tomorrow. You may be like the grasshopper and want to avoid an arduous task, procrastinating because it seems unpleasant or difficult. Or you may feel incapable of doing such a monumental task, so you let self-doubt or insecurity stop you in your tracks. But if you make a habit of putting off mind training practice, your drive to delay doing that task will grow stronger than the drive to act. Unfortunately, the more one delays doing something, the more stress one feels, which further compounds the negative association with the task. Postponing doing what is good for you results in real self-harm. The short-term relief of delaying the task makes procrastination especially insidious because it can result in an unhealthy habit of hesitation.

You can break the procrastination habit through mentally reframing the task. Consider the positive aspects of what you are avoiding. For example, remind yourself of a time when you did something similar and it turned out favorably. Furthermore, remind yourself that there is no time to waste; winter is coming so you mustn't delay. Terrible events like the COVID-19 pandemic come and go, but there is some valuable wisdom in life-threatening events like this. They are clear reminders that your life is brief and will someday end. Don't let death be like a test you didn't study for; now is the time to make the changes needed to be able to reach the end of your life without regrets. As we have seen, mind training is a powerful tool to help you make those changes and handle the stresses and hardship in your life; this chapter will go over some preliminary information to help ensure your mind training sessions go well.

## PRACTICE BEGINS WITH A GOOD MOTIVE

Preparation begins with practices that help you gain insight into using and trusting in your innate wisdom and compassion. This is very important! Some days mind training practice will go well. On other days, you cannot seem to concentrate or develop insight at all. When this happens, you need to change the focus of your contemplative practice and start analyzing the motive behind your practice. For mind training to progress well, you need an altruistic intention, made from the heart. That's why before engaging in a mind training practice, you need to take the time to make your intention good. Creating an intention for your practice is called "setting your motivation." If a motive is based on self-cherishing or GAS, you must adjust it to a benevolent intention. It's similar to an intention you set in daily life; when you brush your teeth, you intend to apply care, and you hope for health and well-being. If you don't brush because you are getting neglectful, you must reset your motivation back to a caring one. When training the mind, the motivation to develop a wise mind and a kind heart is the foundation of a fruitful practice. That is why I invite you to make your motivation based on the four immeasurables, a central concept in my tradition. These four wholesome attitudes are immeasurable because they are wishes a practitioner has for innumerable sentient beings. When such pure intentions are directed outward, they help deepen a person's wisdom and open their heart. These four attitudes are immeasurable love, sometimes called loving-kindness; immeasurable compassion; immeasurable sympathetic joy; and immeasurable equanimity, or balanced inner composure.

Immeasurable loving-kindness is a wish for all sentient beings to be truly happy, without exception. Loving-kindness is similar to the pure wish that a loving mother or caregiver has for their child's life. They wish the very best for their kid. They hope for their child's well-being and joy. Their love is unconditional and motivated by their open heart. This sort of attitude is often directed toward people you feel close to. The practice of *immeasurable* loving-kindness, however, asks that you widen your sphere of true caring and share this sort of loving intention toward all the many sentient beings that exist.

The second of the four immeasurables, compassion, is a sincere wish for others to not have to endure the hardship of suffering. Compassion is much like the earnest wish of a loving mother or caregiver for their sick child. They empathize with their kid's suffering and feel a pure hope that they will be free of disease and distress. The practice of *immeasurable* compassion requests that the practitioner take this attitude of wanting to reduce or alleviate another's anguish and direct it toward all sentient beings. When you do this, you not only discourage any feelings of ill will, but you generate the ability to hold people dear.

The third immeasurable, sympathetic joy, is an attitude of genuine delight for the happiness of others. This type of attitude is much like that of a loving mother or caregiver's great pleasure at seeing their child succeed at something they've worked hard for. They feel as though they are sharing the pleasure of their child's triumph. Being able to share the happiness of another's good fortune helps eliminate selfish tendencies and counteracts jealousy. This immeasurable asks you to recognize, appreciate, and share other beings' good fortune and joy.

The last of the four immeasurables, equanimity, is an attitude that is balanced between aversion and clinging or craving. It is an attitude of inner equipoise and is similar to the confident feeling a loving mom or caregiver has for their grown child when they exhibit the maturity and capability of living well independently. Their confidence in their child's adeptness to handle the difficulties in life results in an internal tranquility and emotional stability. They entirely believe in their child's capability to persevere through difficulties, thus are not averse to their independence and do not feel like it's necessary to cling to them. This immeasurable asks that the practitioner generate the wish that all sentient beings experience this sort of imperturbable inner balance and calm impartiality.

## CALM ABIDING FOR CONCENTRATION

In the context of setting out to do a formal mind training practice, once you have squared away the foundational issue of what is driving your practice, then you can begin a session of training. Start with a few minutes of shamatha, or calm abiding, practice. In this meditative practice you concentrate on one thing, like your breath, a sound, or an object that is real or imagined, such as an apple, or perhaps an image of a buddha, if you are so inclined. This focused meditation calms your mind and helps you develop full attention. Calm abiding is a helpful warm-up exercise to prepare your mind to receive the wisdom of further contemplative practices. Shamatha shouldn't be confused with mind training, however. To change your mind and develop indestructible happiness, you must also deeply absorb the messages and insight you receive—not just focus your attention on something. Any healthy discoveries a practitioner generates from contemplative practices should ultimately be used daily, but only when the practitioner is ready. Premature action could hurt your practice, so first train on the level of your mind, rather than immediately putting your insight into action, perhaps unwisely. There are four critical steps to mind training well: a healthy motive, strong focus, wise analysis, and compassionate action. As a word of caution, you mustn't overdo it; pace yourself and apply moderation. Don't be like tender-footed Sona.

## Not Too Tight, Not Too Loose

Sona was the son of a wealthy businessperson who learned the value of moderation. Because he lived in such luxury, he was a delicate and pampered young man. This gentleman spent his days listening to and playing the lute. Rumor has it he lived so luxuriously that he didn't need to use his feet to get around. As a result, hair grew out of his soles. One day, this tender-footed man decided to take a ride into town. While out and about, he heard a sage profess the importance of not getting attached to luxurious, worldly things. The wise man claimed that nonattachment to worldly pleasures is a means to happiness. Sona wanted to be happy, so he walked miles to practice nonattachment with this enlightened being every day. He was so impatiently enthusiastic about practicing for his happiness that his tender feet quickly developed prominent festering blisters from walking such distances. His ardent desire made him long even more for worldly comforts. Just as he was about to give up training his mind, the sage explained Sona's problems with the practice. "Since you're a musician that enjoys playing the lute, I was wondering if you could tell me, did you produce good music when the lute was tuned just right?"

"Oh, yes," replied Sona. The sage asked, "What if the strings were too tight?" "Then I couldn't play at all, sage," Sona replied. Again the sage asked, "What if the strings were too slack?" The eager student replied, "I couldn't play the lute in that state, either."

"I hope this helps you see why you didn't experience happiness from renouncing worldly luxuries, Sona," the sage concluded. "You can't make a tune sound right if the strings are too loose or tight. Stop trying so hard. Take a relaxed attitude toward practice, but don't slack off." Sona tried again and experienced great results.

## MEDITATION IN MODERATION

Please don't overextend yourself in your practice; otherwise, there is a danger that you might give it up altogether. When it comes to contemplative or analytical meditation, even investigation should be done in moderation. Inquiry into the truth of what is helpful is vital, but once you have a solid insight into how things are, stop the research and put what you've learned into action. There is no need to continue examining and cross-examining the points if you have developed insight, especially if you are already using what you've learned. Refrain from getting mixed up like the confused apple picker in the following story.

Baffled Ben loved to investigate. He was the kind of person who was always curious about everything. One day, Ben found a job picking apples in an apple orchard. When he arrived for work, his boss gave him one small basket and one large one and told him to put the big apples in the big basket and the small apples in the small basket. When the boss came back to check on him at the end of the day, he was shocked to see that both big and small baskets were utterly empty! Angrily, he asked the man, "All I told you to do was put the big apples in the big basket and the small apples in the small basket, but both baskets are empty! Didn't you pick even one apple?" Ben replied, "I understood your instructions perfectly. You told me to put the big apples in the big basket and the small apples in the small basket. There's no problem with that. But, you see, what about medium-sized apples? What should I do with those? I have been asking myself that question the whole day!" So, as you can see, this is the problem with knowing where to draw the limit on how much investigation one does. In the end, you can end up with nothing, just like Ben. If all you do is investigate, there's no room for practical application, and there is the danger of wasting a lot of time. In other words, you can't just talk the talk; you must walk the walk. This type of analytical mind training is a powerfully transformative practice when done successfully for a long time. Set your motive, use calm abiding to focus the mind, analyze the point to completion, then apply the insight you've gained to your life. Challenge yourself, use your intellect, persevere, and have some faith in the process. When you walk the path with a wise mind and a kind heart, it will make a massive difference in your life and the lives of others.

## Reflection

Once upon a time, in a previous lifetime, the Buddha was born as a tiny quail. He had little feet and tiny wings. He could not yet walk or fly. His parents worked very hard building a warm nest to keep him safe and drumming up food to nourish their precious little baby. Throughout his young life, they always tried to keep him warm, safe, and well-fed. One day a fire broke out in the forest. All but the little quail's parents fled to safety. They chose to stay behind and watch over their little one. But the fire got too close; they had no other choice but to sadly fly away to safety. The little quail felt so alone. He watched the surrounding forest fire rage out of control. His mind was overwhelmed with helplessness. He couldn't fly, walk, or do anything to save his body. "All that I have left is my mind," he thought. So, he used his mind, recalling his unselfish parents who generously fed him, kept him warm, watched over him, and risked their lives to stay with him as long as they could. Full of gratitude, the little bird wished all things wholesome and good for his loving parents. It was then that a miracle happened. His wish began to grow. It grew and grew, passing from lifetime to lifetime, until he became a buddha with the thought, "May all beings who are still trapped in the fire of delusion be free of the searing flames of suffering forever." The point of this story is that a wholesome motive can save the world. When you practice the four immeasurables, you are generating a wholesome wish—a hope to end suffering. When practiced regularly, this pure motive will grow over time, mature, and bring immeasurable benefits to immeasurable beings, including yourself.

To practice the four immeasurables, upon waking, sit tall but comfortably and spend a few minutes practicing calm abiding. Focus on your breath, counting each full breath until you reach the count of twenty-five. Recite the first wish of the four immeasurables in your mind, or out loud if you prefer: *May I and all beings have happiness and the cause of happiness.* Take a moment to ponder your wish of loving-kindness. Consider the wish a loving mother or caregiver has for their dear child, a hope they are blessed with unconditional love and genuine acceptance from others. Extend this attitude to all sentient beings and to yourself. Recite the second wish: *May I and all beings be free of suffering and the cause of suffering.* Spend a little while pondering your second wish of compassion. Consider the wish a loving mother or caregiver has for their dear child's well-being: an earnest hope for their sick child to get better. Extend this caring wish to all sentient beings, including yourself. Next recite the wish for the third immeasurable: *May I and all beings never be disassociated from supreme happiness, which is without suffering.* Spend a little time pondering the third immeasurable, sympathetic joy. Consider the wish a loving mother or caregiver has for their dear child, the hope to share the joy of their child's success and good fortune. Extend this caring wish to all sentient beings, including yourself. Extend this same joy to all sentient beings, including yourself. Lastly, recite the wish for the fourth immeasurable: *May I and all beings remain in boundless equanimity, free from both attachment and aversion.* Spend a moment pondering your fourth wish. Recall a mom or caregiver's full confidence in their grown child's ability to handle life's hardships such that it results in an unshakable inner equipoise. Extend this wish for equanimity to all sentient beings, including yourself. Take the wholesome attitude of the four immeasurables with you throughout your day.

# CHAPTER 11

# Practice:
# Guidelines for Mind Training

WHAT FOLLOWS are the guidelines for setting up your mind training practice. When you begin, start by setting aside approximately twenty or more minutes twice a week to practice. Try to associate this practice with something you already habitually do, which will make it easier for you to establish a new habit. For example, aim to practice upon waking in the morning or prior to going to bed.

Ideally, find a quiet space to practice. Sit tall and strong but relaxed. Remember to keep your body, mind, and the practice itself not too tight, not too loose—like the strings of a lute.

## 1. SET A HEALTHY MOTIVATION

While taking into consideration the impermanence and interdependence of yourself and all conscious beings, regard the development of a wise mind and kind heart as your highest aim. Develop a wholesome wish for all sentient beings, including yourself, based on the four immeasurables, which are (1) loving-kindness, (2) compassion, (3) sympathetic joy, and (4) equanimity.

1. May I and all beings have happiness and the cause of happiness.
2. May I and all beings be free of suffering and the cause of suffering.
3. May I and all beings never be disassociated from the supreme happiness, which is without suffering.

4. May I and all beings remain in boundless equanimity, free from both attachment and aversion.

## 2. DEVELOP FOCUS

Briefly practice calm abiding meditation to focus your mind. Count your breaths, counting the inhalation and exhalation as one full breath, up to twenty-five, then repeat. When your mind wanders, gently redirect it back to your breath. Counting out loud will help if you are overly distracted. Do this until your mind is relatively calm; I suggest for about five minutes.

## 3. WISE ANALYSIS

Do a session of contemplative mind training in the following order:
1. Spend some time reading one of the eight points and its commentary from the next chapter of this book. Practice these points in sequential order, one per session.
2. Gently turn your mind back to reflecting on the point if it wanders.
3. Contemplate each point to completion. Your time frame for pondering a point is entirely up to you, but the suggested time is no less than ten to fifteen minutes.
   - Ponder what emotional and mental benefits are produced by thinking or feeling this way.
   - Consider what disadvantages there are to not thinking or feeling this way.
4. Trust and listen to your mind to provide the necessary insight for healthy transformation.

## 4. COMPASSIONATE ACTION

Apply what you've learned by putting it into practice in your daily life. Remember to practice on the level of the mind first; warm-hearted actions will come after your practice matures. This is very important!

If it helps, keep a meditation journal highlighting what you've learned.

# CHAPTER 12

# Practice: Verses for Developing a Wise Mind and a Kind Heart

THE FOLLOWING VERSES for mind training are my own modern rendering of the *Eight Verses of Training the Mind* by the Tibetan master Geshe Langri Tangpa. The original verses are very well known in Tibetan Buddhism. The eight points here are intended to be meditated on and offer a powerful transformative method to change an unhappy, selfish attitude into a joyous one—by generating wisdom and compassion in your heart and mind. This modern world is heavily focused on what is best for the individual alone, even if it is at the expense of others. That's why the aim of these points is to discourage habitual self-concern and encourage concern for other conscious beings, too. It's crucial to meditate on these points using the instructions provided in the previous chapter and keep them in mind as you go about your day. You needn't act on these verses; instead, you should first generate an altruistic attitude on the level of your mind. None of the practices in these verses can hurt you, although they will hurt an inflated ego. So, if you feel some discomfort, it is a sign that your practice is going well. Since you stand in the way of your own happiness, this is a method to get out of your own way so you can directly experience a positive transformation.

**1.** *Every* sentient being is invaluable to you because it is through them that you can generate a mature, healthy mental and emotional disposition.

You want to be happy and free of suffering. But how do you achieve such a thing? Ironically, it is not something that happens when you pursue solely your own satisfaction. You are a being that is in constant relationship because you rely on this world and on other sentient beings. Doesn't it stand to reason that this principal aspect of your reliance plays a part in your happiness as well? To truly get this, you first must develop some wisdom of how things are. Recall the precious knowledge of your interdependence. Realize that you are dependent on this world for everything, and the world is dependent on you. Let go of the perspective that is just based on yourself, what you want, and what others can do for you. If someone does good things for you, they are friends, and you are satisfied; if they do bad things to you, they are enemies, and you are dissatisfied. Judgments like this cause you to ride an emotional roller coaster. You will always encounter a mixture of pleasant and unpleasant behaviors. Let that be a great opportunity to mature and strengthen your mind and heart. That is why it's best to consider everyone as worthy of your kindness, *especially* those who make you feel jealousy, anger, or dislike. Since these disturbing emotions are in your mind, you can learn to exercise some control over them. Training your mind to think in this way about others may feel uncomfortable because it is a direct assault on your self-centered nature. But thanks to others, you can transform mental and emotional negativity into joy by generating goodwill. Having this intention, or motivation, to be genuinely warm-hearted and kind and to benefit others is a cause for happiness. That's what makes other beings so extremely precious. It is through them that you can generate a healthy state of mind and a big warm heart.

## 2.

To end your delusive self-cherishing, humble yourself by envisioning that you are below all other sentient beings.

When you are around others, you probably find yourself comparing yourself with them. Who comes out on top? Do you share your knowledge and talk about your accolades and adventures to boost your ego? Now that you know how significant others are to your well-being, resist the temptation to indulge in your selfish tendencies. But reversing your selfish nature so that you can adopt a healthier, humbler approach to life takes vigilant awareness and hard work! Even monks trained to provide selfless service are challenged doing this. Once, two senior monks were arguing over who was more knowledgeable and could help people the most. A young monk overheard this silly spat and said, "A noncompetitive worm is more knowledgeable than either of you!" That ended that argument. Some monks even take pride in being the most senior monastic, so they compare their ages and years of practice with other monks.

It's essential to consider the areas where you exhibit the strongest sense of pride. Your arrogance, superiority, and competitive nature prevent you from the growth necessary to move forward on the path to joy. To advance toward liberation from suffering, use all your interactions as an opportunity to mentally and emotionally mature. Envision yourself below other conscious beings, even below a worm, which in some ways is more innocent and less conniving than you are. At first, this may bruise your ego—but that is what you want to happen. In reality, nothing terrible is happening to you; this is a mental exercise, and your conditioned sense of superiority is being challenged. As your mind opens to the idea that you are not better than others, there is less ego to get bruised. You'll gradually become wiser through humility. You'll develop a more compassionate understanding for others and, as a result, acquire a healthier disposition.

**3.** At all times, watch your mind for self-cherishing and GAS. The moment you encounter it, label it, and then actively apply the antidote.

How do you feel when you are angry or jealous? Such negative, destructive emotions are agitating to both you and others. They might provoke you to engage in unwholesome mental, physical, or verbal activity that can result in devastating consequences. It's imperative to remain vigilant of your selfish nature and GAS. Behind all destructive emotions is selfishness, the thought of "I," "me," "mine" before anything else. Therefore, remain mindful of your feelings and behavior, then apply the antidote at the first sign of self-centered thoughts or GAS. For example, when looking through your social media feed, if you feel jealous of your friends' achievements, promptly log out of your account. That way, you don't let the afflictive emotion spur you into behaving or thinking in a way that you'll later regret.

When watching the news, if you recognize that you're generating anger toward a particular party or politician, turn it off. Politics have a way of agitating people. It makes people wonder if politicians are using their brains, and if maybe they need a better brain. I'm joking, of course; but what is not a joke is the anger you feel over such people. The moment you start feeling agitated, immediately divert your attention. Be watchful of your selfish thoughts and reactive emotions. If you feel the slightest irritability, be still like a tree, don't say or do anything other than focus on your breath, then apply the antidotes. The antidotes are as follows:

Selfishness: Consider yourself below other beings.

Greed: Focus on what you have, not what you lack.

Anger: Divert your attention to your breath and/or look up and sky gaze. With each out-breath, envision letting go of all that agitation into the wide-open, receptive sky.

Stupidity or ignorance: Remind yourself that nothing lasts forever, and everything changes.

4. When encountering cruel or hapless people, refuse to harden or weaken your heart. Instead, regard these suffering beings as precious and in desperate need of your compassion.

Do you avoid or ignore encounters with people you consider unpleasant? Do you consider yourself better than them? Are they unworthy of your caring attention? How do you feel when you see a homeless encampment or someone asking for money on the street? I find that apart from wanting a home, the homeless population would like to be treated with respect and kindness. They have a story to tell and want to be heard. They desperately need understanding and compassion, yet so many avoid destitute people altogether, as if they are invisible. We tend to avoid people who are overwhelmed with negativity or suffering because we are too busy thinking about our own welfare. There are times when it is wise to steer clear of people who might harm or hurt you, of course, but that is often not what you are doing. This avoidant attitude is generated from a sense of superiority that, over time, weakens your heart. Every time you steer clear of unpleasant people, you risk becoming desensitized. These people were born innocent, just like you, but over time they encountered hardships and tragedies that drove them to behave in ways you find displeasing. Same with those who act cruelly or unjustly. These burdensome people are valuable to your growth. They challenge your fortitude, because patience isn't patience unless it's tested. Therefore, the adversity you may encounter when dealing with difficult people is like weight training. It offers you an opportunity to build your mind and heart muscle. When you consider difficult people as valuable as precious gems, you're able to generate gratitude when you encounter them—or at least a feeling of acceptance, because it's like getting a free gym workout. Adversity is an invaluable occasion to train your mind away from self-preoccupation and toward building inner resilience. With regular practice you learn to handle things that challenge your equanimity by transforming your irritability into caring. Remember, you are working with your mind; you needn't engage verbally or physically, especially if you feel threatened.

5. If you don't react to or get offended by mistreatment, you won't respond in the same unkind way. Mentally take the loss and give them the victory.

This is one of the most critical points of all. It is also very challeng-ing to do. When people sling unkind criticism or insults toward you, do you immediately become defensive and fight or flee? This is the typical reaction. People are highly self-protective. However, this prac-tice challenges that part of you that is attached to your beliefs about yourself. It asks you to remain humble even under verbal attack and let your attacker win the battle. That way, you do not succumb to the same unkind behavior, but instead choose peace. This does not mean that you should be a doormat. If you have been mistreated and it results in actual loss, it is your right to seek justice. For example, I once had a student who was cheated out of a significant amount of money. He asked me whether he should take the loss or seek lit-igation. I told him that this practice is something you do with your mind. If the attack is not just verbal but physical, then it is wiser and more compassionate to protect yourself. The point of taking the loss is to challenge your attachment to winning. All your life, you've day-dreamed of winning and have felt the sting of disappointment. Yet you continue to dream of things like having a nice car, or a beauti-ful house, great clothes, and expensive gadgets. But how often do you think about others gaining these nice things instead? This mind training practice urges you to let go of being the big shot. On the level of mind, let the other person have the success and allow your-self to lose the stress.

# 6.

Consider the betrayal of people that you've had hope for and have helped as a means to practice wisdom and compassion. See them as great spiritual teachers.

When you've grown close to a person you've helped, like a relative, friend, or coworker, how does it feel when they suddenly betray you? You likely feel angry toward that person because they are not grateful for all you've done to help them. It is painful when trusted people repay your kindness with mistreatment. Furthermore, the more you love them, the more it hurts. Most people react to this scenario by withdrawing their love and replacing it with hurt or even hatred. But by doing so, they are making a grave mistake and resorting to love based on desire.

At my monastery, Thangkar Dechen Choling, we understand the true challenge of keeping your love and compassion unconditional. We provide housing, accommodations, and free education for many orphans. The staff and I work tirelessly to feed, care for, educate, support, and parent them. It is challenging work! Quite often, the team has sleepless nights caring for sick children. They change soiled sheets, clean up vomit, and comfort them through the process. Even though these orphans are at a disadvantage, some of them are excellent students and show their wholehearted commitment to the path. We all put enormous hope in the ones that show the most enthusiasm. Occasionally, one of these orphans we hoped for will run away. Consequently, we all experience shock and dismay. At moments like this, it's crucial that we not cave in to reactive negativity. We recognize that the strength of our loving hearts is being tested. So how do we pass the test? We transform negativity into positivity, which you must do when encountering the same. Mentally recognize your "traitor" as a great spiritual teacher who is testing your resolve to follow the path of wisdom and compassion. Considering it this way, you can see that they are helping your heart and mind strengthen and mature. They are assisting in the cultivation of your patience and compassion. You can even transform your enemies into friends using this tool.

7. When you encounter suffering beings, consider them invaluable to your practice. Secretly envision absorbing their pain and giving them an antidote to what harms them.

In chapter 5, you engaged in the practice of *tonglen*, or taking and giving. This visualization exercise helps you stop indulging in self-obsessive thoughts so you can start generating compassion for those conscious beings you encounter who are exhibiting pain and misery. This practice is not just something you do while meditating. You can develop an instant practice of taking and giving when you run across those that are actively suffering in your daily life, whether near or far. For example, suppose you hear someone you are acquainted with at work is struggling with an illness. In that case, you can envision taking the virus, transforming it inside you, then giving them helpful antibodies for healing. As a word of caution, it is essential to keep this practice from serving as an ego boost. Don't develop a savior complex. Since this is a mental exercise, you aren't actually taking away someone's suffering. You are simply envisioning doing so in order to grow the seed of your compassion and weed out selfishness. This practice may cause discomfort as it destabilizes your attachment to selfish impulses and helps you mature. The better you get at tonglen, the more you stand to gain. To assist with these growing pains, remind yourself that you aren't genuinely consuming their suffering. You're only visualizing taking the suffering away to grow your heart. When done right, this practice is empowering, not detrimental. Start with people you care for, then move to those you feel neutral toward, then try it on those conscious beings you dislike. I'm not too fond of crocodiles. However, the practice of taking and giving has made me dislike them a little less.

8. Base this practice on wisdom and compassion, not craving and aversion. Don't attach to what your mind has made or label independent things as good or bad; consider them illusions that can help you develop joy.

Contemplate whether you are practicing mind training to develop wisdom and compassion, or whether you have a more selfish intention to train your mind in order to gain something good or avoid something you're averse to. As you now know, the precious knowledge of our mutual dependence helps you to see that everything is connected, so striving for your own benefit does not make good sense. Wouldn't it be best to generate an intention to honor your interconnectedness by engaging responsibly in the world? The world is a fleeting experience, something we know because nothing lasts forever and because it is something that you encounter through your mind. You also know that things like a GASSY state of mind, deeply conditioned memories, self-deception, and self-absorption contribute to a negative point of view. In contrast, hope, self-belief, determination, insight into the truth, caring, and sharing generate a positive perspective. Although people have labeled things so we have shared terms everyone can agree on—we all know what a "watch" or a "house" is—each person uniquely perceives and judges these things. This judgment is based on each individual's encounters, thoughts, senses, feelings, perceptions, and awareness. Multiple factors, causes, and conditions work together to influence your viewpoint of what is "good" or "bad." Considering all these variables, existence is more like a mental projection or dream if you analyze it. When you are aware that you are in something like a dream, you can enjoy it. You know that the dream may seem frightening sometimes, but it can't really hurt you unless you allow it to. Thinking this way is liberating, because it gives you two channels you can switch back and forth between. You are both aware of how things appear on the surface, and you are aware of the more profound truth of how things really are: our mutual dependence. Either way, your perception is created by your mind. Strive to train it so that you'll enjoy a life benefited by a wise mind and a kind heart. This will enable you to live strong and happy.

# CHAPTER 13

# Takeaway Practice

T HE VERY MOMENT you encounter a problem, don't just react, act. Choose joy! The following condensed mind training practice is one you can commit to memory and take with you to put to use anywhere, anytime, whenever you encounter some difficulty.

1. **Healthy Motivation**. Recall your interdependence and the wishes based on the four immeasurables: loving-kindness, compassion, sympathetic joy, and equanimity.

2. **Strong Focus**. Briefly observe the natural inhalation and exhalation of your breath to focus your mind.

3. **Wise Analysis**. Investigate what is problematic and why. Are you asking, "Why me?" Is your self-absorption or GAS the cause of the problem? What have you learned from this book that can help you solve the problem in this moment?

4. **Compassionate Action**. After a little thoughtful analysis of the problem, use one of the helpful solutions that you've learned from your mind training practice. In life we are all given the choice to either impulsively react or consciously act. If you become frustrated with someone, you have a choice: you can choose anger or choose to act compassionately. Consider their suffering, and imagine that you take the loss and give them the victory. Resist reacting and instead choose to consider them a great spiritual teacher, testing your resolve to remain openhearted. When faced with difficulties, you can either act selfishly, turn a blind eye to your problems, and fall deeper into ignorance, or you can align yourself with a

compassionate view, act wisely, and move closer to awakening. When you learn to wisely rise above your selfish nature and genuinely act out of care for others' happiness and well-being, your mind and heart open to joy.

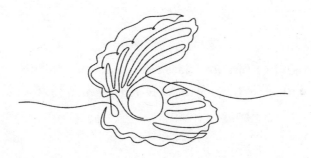

"My manifold aspirations have given rise to humiliating criticism
and suffering, but, having received instructions for taming
the misconception of self, even if I have to die,
I have no regrets."
—GESHE CHEKAWA

# Acknowledgments

In this interdependent world, all things rely on other things to exist. There are many people I owe gratitude to, as this book would not exist at all if it weren't for them. I'd like to first express my appreciation to you, the reader. Without you, there would be no point in writing this book. And of course, this book wouldn't exist if it weren't for the many folks affiliated with Wisdom Publications. I genuinely appreciate Dr. Nicholas Ribush, one of the founders of Wisdom Publications, who helped open the door for me to this wonderful publishing company. Once the doors were opened, Tara Buddhist Center's Paloma Garcia arranged a meeting with Daniel Aitken, the CEO of Wisdom Publications. Without Paloma and Daniel's help, this manuscript might have sat in a pile of manuscripts, gathering dust. Due to their support, it reached Wisdom Publications' editorial and production manager, Laura Cunningham. She was the one who saw this work's potential, a potential that wouldn't exist without the Dipkar Institute for Vajrayana team members Sandy Pham, Tatiana Friar, Jules Jallab, and Jill Walter. My Dipkar team helped me with organization, research, and development. Upon completion, developmental editor Philip Rappaport and Wisdom Publications' editor Brianna Quick helped me polish the manuscript. I sincerely appreciate everyone and everything that came together to make this book possible.

# References

Begley, Sharon. 2007a. "The Brain: How the Brain Rewires Itself." *Time*. January 19, 2007. https://content.time.com/time/magazine/article/0,9171, 1580438,00.html.
———. 2007b. *Train Your Mind, Change Your Brain*. New York: Penguin Random House.
Bonneh, Y.S., A. Cooperman, and D. Sagi. 2001. "Motion-Induced Blindness in Normal Observers." *Nature* 411.6839: 798–801. doi: 10.1038/35081073.
Cerretani, Jessica. 2011. "The Contagion of Happiness. Harvard Researchers Are Discovering How We Can All Get Happy." *Harvard Medicine* (Summer 2011). https://magazine.hms.harvard.edu/articles/contagion-happiness.
Fifer, Jordan. 2022. "Statistics Expert Says Consider the Odds Ahead of Friday's Mega Million Lottery." Virginia Tech News. July 28, 2022. https://news.vt .edu/articles/2022/07/mediarelations-lotteryjackpot.html.
Frankl, Viktor E. 1962. *Man's Search for Meaning: An Introduction to Logotherapy*. Boston: Beacon Press.
Heruka, Tsangnyön. 2010. *The Life of Milarepa*. Translated by Andrew Quintman. New York: Penguin Books.
Jiang, Jingjing. 2018. "How Teens and Parents Navigate Screen Time and Device Distractions." Pew Research Center. August 22, 2018. https://www.pewresearch .org/internet/2018/08/22/how-teens-and-parents-navigate-screen-time -and-device-distractions/.
Marchant, Jo. 2016. *Cure: A Journey into the Science of Mind Over Body*. New York: Broadway Books.
Nierenberg, Cari. 2017. "The Strange 'McGurk' Effect: How Your Eyes Can Affect What You Hear." Live Science. February 28, 2017. https://www.live science.com/58047-mcgurk-effect-weird-way-eyes-trick-brain.html.
NPR. 2010. "Bet You Didn't Notice 'the Invisible Gorilla.'" *Talk of the Nation*. May 19, 2010. https://www.npr.org/2010/05/19/126977945/bet-you-didnt -notice-the-invisible-gorilla.
Newberg, Andrew, and Mark Robert Waldman. 2012. *Words Can Change Your Brain*. New York: Penguin Random House.

Pabongka Rinpoche. 1997. *Liberation in the Palm of Your Hand*. Translated by Michael Richards. Boston: Wisdom Publications.

Parker, Clifton B. 2015. "Embracing Stress is More Important than Reducing Stress, Stanford Psychologist Says." *Stanford News*. May 7, 2015. https://news .stanford.edu/2015/05/07/stress-embrace-mcgonigal-050715/.

Park, Soyoung Q., Thorsten Kahnt, Azade Dogan, Sabrina Strang, Ernst Fehr, and Philippe N. Tobler. 2017. "A Neural Link between Generosity and Happiness." *Nature Communications* 8. https://doi.org/10.1038/ncomms15964.

Radin, Dean, Nancy Lund, Masaru Emoto, and Takashige Kizu. 2009. "Effects of Distant Intention on Water Crystal Formation: A Triple-Blind Replication." *Journal of Scientific Exploration* 22.4. https://www.researchgate.net/publica tion/268983842_Double-blind_test_of_the_Effects_of_Distant_Intention _on_Water_Crystal_Formation.

Shackell, Erin M., and Lionel G. Standing. 2007. "Mind Over Matter: Mental Training Increases Physical Strength." *North American Journal of Psychology* 9.1 (March 2007): 189–200. https://www.researchgate.net/pub lication/241603526_Mind_Over_Matter_Mental_Training_Increases_Physi cal_Strength.

Shantideva. 2006. *The Way of the Bodhisattva*. Translated by Padmakara Translation Group. Boston: Shambhala Publications.

Singh, Maanvi. 2014. "Food Psychology, How to Trick your Palate into a Tastier Meal." NPR. December 21, 2014. https://www.npr.org/sections/thesalt /2014/12/31/370397449/food-psychology-how-to-trick-your-palate-into-a -tastier-meal.

Spanner, Holly. n.d. "What's the Smallest Particle?" BBC Science Focus. Accessed August 19, 2023. https://www.sciencefocus.com/science/what s-the-smallest-particle/.

Sun, Sai, Ziqing Yao, Jaixin Wei, and Rongiun Yu. 2015. "Calm and Smart? A Selective Review of Meditation Effects on Decision Making." *Frontiers in Psychology* 6:1059 (July 24, 2015). doi: 10.3389/fpsyg.2015.01059.

Szabo, Attila, and Katey L. Hopkinson. 2007. "Negative Psychological Effects of Watching the News in the Television: Relaxation or Another Intervention May Be Needed to Buffer Them." *International Journal of Behavioral Medicine* 14.2: 57–62. doi: 10.1007/BF03004169.

Tolstoy, Leo. 1993. *War and Peace*. Translated by Louise Maude and Aylmer Maude. Wordsworth Classics. Hertsfordshire, UK: Wordsworth Editions.

Tzu, Sun. 2000. *Sun Tzu on the Art of War*. Translated by Lionel Giles. Leicester, England: Allandale Online Publishing.

Wegner, Daniel M. 1989. *White Bears and Other Unwanted Thoughts: Suppression, Obsession, and the Psychology of Mental Control*. New York: Viking.

Weir, Kirsten. 2014. "The Lasting Impact of Neglect." *Monitor on Psychology* 45.6 (June 2014). https://www.apa.org/monitor/2014/06/neglect.

# Index

*Way of the Bodhisattva, The* (Shantideva), 62, 87
Wegner, Daniel, 113
wholesome behavior, 54, 55, 69, 85
"why me" thinking, 7–8, 19, 37
wisdom
   compassion and, 144–47, 177
   development of, 54, 61–63

importance of, 55
selflessness and, 124
wise analysis as, 166, 179
words, power of, 132
*Words Can Change Your Brain* (Newberg, Waldman), 132

# About the Author

His Eminence Khangser Rinpoche was born in Kathmandu, Nepal, in May 1975. At five years of age, a search party positively identified him as the reincarnation of the seventh Khangser Rinpoche. He is one of three high lamas responsible for recognizing the rebirth of the spiritual leader of Tibet, His Holiness the Dalai Lama. Khangser Rinpoche completed his preliminary study of Buddhist philosophy at the Institute of Buddhist Dialectics in Dharamshala, India. He later went on to advanced Buddhist studies in sutra and tantra at Sera Jey Monastery and Gyuto Tantric Monastic University. It was there he earned the *geshe lharampa* degree and a doctorate degree in tantra, both with the highest honors in the top division. Khangser Rinpoche presently serves as vice abbot of Gyuto Monastery and as the founder and administrative head of Thangkar Dechen Choling Monastic Institute. This institute is both a monastery and a school, and generously provides food, housing, and education in both Dharma and contemporary Western curricula to over eighty young monks in Nepal. The entire student population comes from impoverished conditions, and many of them are orphans. Khangser Rinpoche has established many Dipkar centers around the globe, spearheading philanthropic efforts such as providing free food to those in need. He also established the Dipkar Vajrayana Institute to offer free Dharma education to all who wish to learn. Khangser Rinpoche is considered one of the great Buddhist teachers of the modern age. He has dedicated his entire life to providing spiritual medicine for what ails a broken spirit. He believes his mission is to help as many suffering beings as possible.

# What to Read Next
# from Wisdom Publications

**The Compassionate Life**
His Holiness the Dalai Lama

"This sorely needed prescription for sanity and kindness in the world is unbelievably simple and unbelievably important, and therefore a practice worthy of our wholehearted commitment." —Jon Kabat-Zinn, author of *Wherever You Go, There You Are*

**Transforming Problems into Happiness**
Lama Zopa Rinpoche

"A masterfully brief statement of Buddhist teachings on the nature of humanity and human suffering . . . This book should be read as the words of a wise, loving parent." —*Utne Reader*

**Essential Mind Training**
*Tibetan Classics, Volume 1*
Thupten Jinpa

"Anyone intrigued by the potential to bend our minds in the direction of greater clarity and kindness will find great satisfaction in *Essential Mind Training*." —Daniel Goleman, author of *Emotional Intelligence*

**The Attention Revolution**
*Unlocking the Power of the Focused Mind*
Alan Wallace
Foreword by Daniel Goleman

"Indispensable for anyone wanting to understand the mind. A superb, clear set of exercises that will benefit everyone." —Paul Ekman, Professor Emeritus at University of California San Francisco, and author of *Telling Lies* and *Emotions Revealed*